EURO 2004

2004

PORTUGAL

The TOTAL GUIDE

Lloyd Pettiford

ARCTURUS

Arcturus Publishing Ltd
26/27 Bickels Yard
151–153 Bermondsey Street
London SE1 3HA

Published in association with
foulsham
W. Foulsham & Co. Ltd,
The Publishing House, Bennetts Close, Cippenham,
Slough, Berkshire SL1 5AP, England

ISBN 0-572-02971-3

British Library Cataloguing-in-Publication Data: a catalogue record for
this book is available from the British Library

Design by Alex Ingr

Printed in Italy

Contents

Acknowledgements

Given the uncertainty over England's qualification until the very last minute and the fact that I have a real job, this book was written in double quick time to ensure that it was available to you in plenty of time for the tournament. Accordingly, these acknowledgements are being hastily written at the last moment and I fear I may miss out those who should be mentioned. If I do I apologise. On the other hand, I am remembering to thank (in no particular order) Matthew Smith, David Harding, Caroline Arnold, Ronan Fitzsimons, Tom Mitchell, Steve Kneller and all the other Midlands and Black Sea Saints, William for cheering me up after the cup final, Paul Whittle and all the usual suspects. This book was written without the aid of an EU research grant and with very little opportunity actually to re-read any of it before publication.

Dedication

I suppose you come to realise in life you must protect love to survive, and in the process to observe some purpose after all, some purpose after all...

For a change this book is not dedicated to Matthew Le Tissier, though my appreciation of his talent remains undimmed, but instead to The Family Cat in the hope that they will reform for a one-off gig, perhaps in The Rescue Rooms in Nottingham?

Introduction

Turn Right At Madrid

The European Football Championships...is it an enigma inside a dilemma atop a mystery wrapped around a cunning riddle? Or is it a mockery of a travesty of a sham of a farce? Well possibly.... Certainly it is, very much, a far, far cry from small boys in the park, jumpers for goalposts, um, isn't it? For some, the absence of hopeless minnows such as Costa Rica, Peru, and Iran (or the Faroe Islands) means that the European Championships are the most important of sporting competitions and much more difficult to win than the World Cup. For others they are an appalling waste of time; the embarrassing 'baby-brother' filling the gaps – though in most unsatisfactory fashion it must be said – between the real business of '*el mundial*' (apologies for the occasional lapse into Spanish during this book, but we're all European now, my siesta-loving, schnapps-quaffing, garlic-drinking friends).

For others, however, the European Championships are something else entirely. For Mr Maxwell R. Deakin of Colston Bassett, Nottinghamshire (a heating engineer with a passion for Notts County and strong cheese) for instance, his brain addled by decades of using and abusing the heady aroma of the local Stilton, the European Football Championships represent a small boiled fruit sweet in orbit somewhere around Jupiter. And why not? This is, after all, more sense than we are used to from the President of the world's most powerful country these days. But since they have now locked him up (Max not Dubya alas!), let's give that argument no more of our attention.

Many people in England, given the (English) team's quite reasonable record in World Cups, tend to fall into the camp that pays rather less attention to the Euro footy Champs. This is, I believe, a very serious error of judgement, and not simply because 'mickey mouse' cups always become more important once you get to the final and win it – as England are almost certain to do this time. No, it is also a mistake to ignore Euro-footy for other reasons. First, lots of very interesting things happen at Euro-tournaments. The Germans get beaten on penalties for one. The Germans get beaten on penalties for one. The Germans get beaten on penalties for one. The Germans get beaten on penalties for one. *[Editor's note: Please enjoy this gratuitously repeated sentence and reread at your leisure until bored.]* And so, four hours later...

Also it (the European Championships in case you were getting lost in anti-German reverie) gets won by teams whose preparation involves – allegedly – lounging around drinking Tuborg Export (remember that? Now served extensively in Romania for what it's worth...) and watching hardcore Scandinavian porn, before going on to beat the Germans in the final, before going on to beat the Germans in the final, before going on to beat the Germans in the final, before going on to beat the Germans in the final etc etc. *[Editor's note: I hope you're not going to over use this literary device? Author's note: Go away, I demand my artistic freedom.]* That happened when Denmark won in 1992 despite initially finishing behind Yugolslavia in qualifying. (More on that story later...)

Alas, the Germans do not always lose, but where they haven't, compensation has often been forthcoming in the form of things like England conceding a goal against Holland. That last sentence can't be right, can it? Ah, I know, it wasn't finished. This is what it should have said: 'Alas the Germans do not always lose, but where they haven't, compensation has often been forthcoming in the form of things like England conceding a goal against Holland...when they were winning 4–0, thus denying Scotland any chance of qualification on goal-difference.' Lest anyone Scottish be reading this – and let's face it, after their German manager led them to finish behind Germany and then to ignominious play-off defeat having finished (just) above the might of Iceland, Lithuania and the Denmark B team, that *is* unlikely – I would just like to stress that life has become so much sweeter since I threw away that childish, imperialist habit of believing you were part of the same country and therefore supporting you. I wish the TV people would also realise that Eire is not part of England, or even of the United Kingdom, either, though in that case the shared Cockney accent of 90% of the team makes the mistake understandable at least. *[Editor's note: Publication schedules mean that that last paragraph – and this note – had to be written before Scotland's play-off loss to Holland. If by some absolute miracle they won, please read the chapter on the qualifying campaign to find out how lucky they were, and then the chapter on the qualifying teams to find out how little chance they have in the finals themselves. But we're pretty confident you'll find Holland instead.] [Author's PS: Oh yes!]*

Now, where were we before all of that nationalistic non-sense? Ah yes, reasons for taking more interest in the European Championships. Well, not only does it fill World Cup 'gaps' (not to mention the summer!) and not only are *we* gonna win it this time and not only do the Germans lose on penalties, but also the whole tournament has, until now, been a giant Euro-conspiracy aimed primarily – though not exclusively, given what happened to poor old Holland in 1984![1] – at England. More shocking than the Common Agricultural Policy (and, maybe, even as interesting) while we have been paying little attention to them, they've been cheating us. Yes, shocking I know, but you should be told, and will be in the pages that follow; pages that tell you all you need to know about the European Championships and how Eng-er-land have been robbed time and time and time and – dare we say it – time again! This time however, with our Europhile PM (he of the patronising European hand gesture, come-on-into-the-Euro-with-me eyebrows) *and* super cool Swede in charge of the football, nothing will stop us.[2]

---

1 Though you will read more on this later, Holland went out on goal-average (not difference) after their chief rivals played their last game after all others had been completed and won 12-1 against a team they had struggled to beat 3-2 away.

In the pages that follow you will find your complete
guide to Euro 2004. In fact, if I do say so myself, it is
something of a bargain: not only is it cheap but it is also
even more complete than some other (so called) complete guides because we offer you – in addition to the
facts themselves – some completely made up stuff which
is put in only because I find it mildly amusing and which
the wilfully negligent publishers are prepared to put up
with rather than to get involved in the irritating and
time-consuming process of investigating the matter further. One thing you may think is made up but, in fact, is
not – because my mate knows someone who knows
Dieter Eilst and he says it's true (and then I read it in *The
Guardian* somewhen[3]) – is that the Germans won Euro
1996[4] because they were allowed two bottles of beer,
brewed according to the strict Teutonic beer purity laws
(*das deutsche Reinheitsgebot*, if you're interested...) of
1516[5]) per night during the tournament.

Anyway, as already alluded to, you will find amongst
the pages within a history of the tournament, detailing
who won and how England have been robbed time and
again. But more, you will go on to marvel at the story of
qualification, not least how Greece achieved it with their
revolutionary 5-5-0 formation. Germany, having almost
not qualified for Japan/Korea (and so arranging a special
'Korea tournament' against pub teams to ensure their
appearance in the final), this time managed to ensure

2 Except possibly France, Spain, Portugal, Germany, Holland, Czech Republic, Croatia, Bulgaria,
Italy, Sweden, Denmark, Switzerland, Latvia etc

3 Please note that in Wiltshire, from whence my wife and uncle hail, the word 'somewhen' is a
perfectly cromulent one.

4 Darn it, at the proof-reading stage I noticed I had inserted 2004 here by mistake! Please no!!!

5 Or sometime around that time...let's face it, who cares??? Do you really think this book was
expensive enough to get that kind of thing checked?

qualification by getting themselves put into the so-called (although very accurately mind you) Group of Super Minnows. Meanwhile, England did glorious and success-ful battle in the so- called Group of 'We've got naughtier fans than you' and Wales in the Group of 'F*** me boyo, we might actually do it this time'. Of course it soon became the group of 'oh shit we might not after all' and then finally...*[Editor's note: Writing in early November the author neglected to up-date this section. Please insert 'became the group of "bloody hell we did make it after all"' if Wales emerge victorious from one of the grimmest countries in Europe – oh and Russia too. On the other hand if defeat arrives as expected please insert 'became the group of "same sh*t different tournament"']*

You will also find details of all 16 finalists (a profile of the teams), including predictions of their overall chances and quick quizzes which mix a combination of brain teasers and humour (and blatant space fillers in the case of Europe's dullest teams). The key players section is not necessarily a 'best player' section, but perhaps the player whose form will do most to determine that country's chances; so this might be the famous striker or midfield general, but might be for instance the Czech Republic's promising young goalkeeper or the player whose domes-tic form has been low for some time but who might get it together for the big occasion (Liverpool's Vlad the Inca-pable or Southampton's Anders 'f crissakes' Svensson, perchance?). Where no one obvious emerges in this cate-gory I will use my extensive powers of imagination in including wild guesses at which 16-year-old you've not even heard of yet will suddenly emerge and sweep all before them.

Just in case you're planning to go to the finals, or even have one of those drunken conversations about going which involve driving down (don't forget to turn right at Madrid), there's a guide to Portugal...based mostly on a mate of mine's trip to Oporto 23 years ago. There's also some handy Portuguese phrases such as 'Hey, that decent one, isn't he really Brazilian?', '5-1 to the Eng-er-land...who'd have thought it...?' and 'Yes please, a little more delicately smoked and sliced ham would go down a treat with this super fine dry sherry' – although in Portuguese, obviously. As well as useful phrases we've broken new 'guide' ground by including useless ones too; these – usually to do with the colour of goats and the price of a bus ticket to Vigo – are designed to help you show what a fantastic command of the language you have. They might come in handy for worrying people on buses and you may wish to try them out if you're after a bit of unpredictability and excitement. And finally, as well as all that there are fiendish quizzes throughout which will test your brain to the limits (providing they are, of course, quite small indeed), a fill-in chart of all the finals groupings (as if you'll ever get around to filling in that – no one ever does do they?) and a sensational, exclusive and mythical cut-out and keep guide to buying the right pair of scissors.

And as if that wasn't enough, then there'll be a sophisticated and accurate conclusion making all kinds of insane predictions. Since it will be the only bit of the book I have the luxury of writing after the draw for the finals are made, it will look at the likely qualifiers from each. How long all this will be I cannot say and God knows what it'll be about. Much depends on how much I can drag out the rest of the book as to how long the predictions will be. *[Editor's note: Ain't that the truth daddy-o! Even in this short introduction how many times has he gratuitously repeated sentences about Germany losing, Germany losing, Germany losing, Germany losing, Germany losing, Germany losing, Germany losing?]* In any case, if you thought the rugby World Cup was good, imagine beating France in the final of this…

Alcohol Quiz

1   *Who won the 1992 European Championships having allegedly prepared with a mixture of Tuborg and Carlsberg?*

2   *Who won the European Championships in 1996 after allegedly preparing with Beck's and Holsten Pils, having a management who allowed them the highest daily intake of beer of any of the competing teams at two bottles?*

3   *Who played like a pub team and didn't win Euro 2000?*

4   *Who famously toasted 'To alcohol! The cause of and solution to…all of life's problems'?*

5   *Alcohol imporves spilling. Ture or Fasle?*

6   *I know the publishers want this by December but wouldn't it be better for me to get some sleep now than keep churning out this drunken drivel?* [Editor's note: You mean you were sober when writing any of this?] [Author's Note: 'Sober'? Now that's a rather grey area…]

Non-Alcohol Quiz

1   *How many stadia have been specifically built for Euro 2004 in Portugal?*

2   *How many stadia will be used in total?*

3 *How much money is estimated to have been spent on the tournament?*

4 *How many of the stadia bear the exotic name 'Municipal'?*

5 *Which of the following should you avoid in Portugal? a) Driving b) Prostitutes c) Being rude to the police d) Fado?*

6 *Was there any real point in this quiz and are the others more interesting?*

The 'Remember That Football Is NOT A Matter of Life and Death' Quiz

1 *How many people were killed in the explosion of a chemical factory in Bhopal, India in 1984? Was it 300, 3,000 or 20,000?*

2 *True or False? In the case of Bhopal requests for extradition of the head of Union Carbide (which ran the factory) has been consistently denied and compensation levels for victims was around $400.*

3 *Ah, but isn't that a lot of money in India?*

4 *What percentage of the world's population live on incomes of around $2 per day or less?*

5 *True or False? Slavery has been abolished.*

6 *In 1988 Iran Air Flight 655 was shot down over the Persian Gulf killing all 290 passengers on board heading for the Islamic holy city of Mecca. Who shot it down?*

7 *Did the US government originally believe that the Lockerbie bombing later that year was a revenge attack for the above?*

8 *But hasn't Libya admitted to doing it?*

9 *How was the captain of the Vincennes punished?*

10 *Do you think you'd find more stuff like this if you actually looked rather than watched CNN and is it any wonder that there is so much anti-US resentment in the world?*

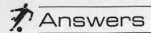

Answers

Alcohol Quiz
1. Denmark – probably
2. Germany
3. England
4. Homer J. Simpson
5. Treu
6. Yes

Non-Alcohol Quiz
1. seven
2. 10
3. £285 million
4. three
5. Probably all four, although Fado is a popular musical form that you ought to try if you're a culture vulture
6. No and Yes

The 'Remember That Football Is NOT A Matter of Life and Death' Quiz
1. Both 3,000 and 20,000. 3,000 was the immediate death toll and 20,000 the number subsequently estimated to have died from related illness and injury
2. True
3. No, even living in miserable poverty that's only about the income of one person for a year
4. About half. That's more than three billion people
5. False. From Sudan to Indonesia through Chinese prisons and illegal operations using illegal immigrants in the USA and UK it is very much still a phenomenon world wide
6. The USS Vincennes 'accidentally'
7. Yes but started to point the finger at Libya when it needed Iranian and Syrian support in the Gulf War
8. Actually they are very careful to say that they are paying compensation to allow them to enter the normal community of nations again
9. How was the captain of the Vincennes punished? He was ultimately decorated by the US government with the Legion of Merit award for 'exceptionally meritorious conduct in the performance of an outstanding service'
10. Yes you would and No it isn't

Conspiracy

The True[6] Story of the European Football Championships 1960–2000

This chapter started out as an idea for a book.
When it became clear there wasn't enough in the idea for a book
it became a chapter. When it became clear that it wasn't such a good idea
for a chapter either, it became this, a history of the European Championships.
There's a few interesting bits and some quizzes at the end. Bear with me.

M any people outside England assume that the English World Cup triumph of 1966 was some kind of Euro (specifically Anglo) fix. Refereeing, have claimed those models of footballing morality and virtue in Argentina and Uruguay,[7] favoured the more robust northern European style, allowing the English and the Germans to contest the final at the expense of silky South American skill. However, this claim hardly

---

6 As Margaret Thatcher once admitted, in a rare moment of self-knowledge, 'truth is a very difficult concept' and so it proves here.

7 The Spanish translation of 'models of football virtue' is 'cabrones sucios' which curiously translates back into English as 'dirty bastards'.

holds up when one considers that fouls certainly were punished – in the England v Argentina game the home team were penalised 36 times to the visitors 19 so they can hardly claim they were unprotected, even if it is true that today Nobby Stiles would be lucky to last 90 seconds, let alone 90 minutes, on the pitch. (This also, you may think, somewhat gives the lie to Sir Alf Ramsey's famous 'animals' claim although he was, in fact, referring to them urinating in the tunnel of Wembley stadium, so he may have had a point).

Such contentions – of English/European bias – actually turn the facts of the matter on their head however. In reality, England won in 1966 precisely because, with the games being played on home soil, we were able to control and stamp out the disgraceful fraud and bias which has prevented England – clearly the best team in the world – winning a major tournament before or since. By the time of the 1996 Europeans, regrettably, Eurocrats had successfully infiltrated the country to the extent that victory was once again impossible. Forget Gazza's stretch and the one that hit the post – if either had gone in it would probably[8] have been disallowed. All will be revealed in the pages that follow but, in short, English football has been starved of success by a Euro-fraud. You are about to read a shocking account of why England has never won the European Championships. It is not only shocking, but also absolutely true.[9] Could there be any other remotely reasonable explanation for our inglorious failure? 'No' I hear you cry, correctly and in unison.

8 Probably is probably, well definitely actually, exaggerating but unless you read footnotes – and let's face it, who does? – you will be blissfully unaware that this whole 'conspiracy' idea is a feeble mix of lies, supposition, innuendo and jingoistic nonsense. Sorry about that.

9 For reasons of space the letters 'un' were removed from this word before publication.

Before we delve into this shocking world, it is worth making the point that despite the British (henceforth 'English' in shamelessly imperial and arrogant fashion) reputation as 'awkward partners' in the European Union, I think we all know where to point the finger. Basically, if the French were not in it we'd have been drinking trappist ales with the Belgians and enjoying red-light districts with the Dutch much more than we have. We'd have been grating cheese that smells like 'sick' on to our pasta for decades and kicking donkeys to death and sleeping all afternoon. We'd watch more porn and eat bigger sausages. Oh yes, if it wasn't for the French we'd have been much more European, and it is with them that much of the initial blame for English failure stems.

It was, after all, General de Gaulle in 1961 who opposed British entry to the EEC, citing as his (infantile, primary school) reason that he didn't like us being friends with the Americans. He didn't stop to think that there might be a reason for this; namely that it is better to be friends with someone you can look down on and get all superior with in their own language than having friends who prefer paint stripper to beer, speak in a series of shrugs and nasal grunts and who think that not wearing deodorant is the 'thing to do' because 'uzzer wize eet clogs ze poorz'. (By the way, this is a football fact and quiz book. Accordingly, please do not expect any non-football facts to actually have been checked. Please do not write to the publishers to point out – for instance – that it wasn't de Gaulle but instead Valery Giscard D'Estaing, even though it wasn't.)[10]

10 Fact: Valery Giscard D'Estaing translated into German and then into English using one of those electronic translator thingys comes out as 'valley of the small snails in loin cloths.' Fact: If you translate Tony Blair into Spanish and then into French using a similar machine it comes out with 'le petit escargot qui porter un cloth de loin.' Strange huh?

However, the small matter of the EEC is not the end of it. In 1958 on an official trip to Britain, General de Gaulle was entrusted with the delivery of England's accepted entry to the first ever European Championships. Reasoning to himself that England ought really to take up baseball if we liked the Americans that much – and no doubt feeling queasy after one too many garlic éclairs for lunch – de Gaulle, however, in yet another demonstration of pointless spite, never passed on the invitation. England – who would obviously have won – were never in the tournament. The very idea, by the way, that England's absence had anything to do with our own arrogance is clearly very silly indeed.

Obviously tarnished by England's absence the tournament went ahead in any case, although presumably there was much debate as to whether there was any point. And it was won by the USSR after a 2-1 extra-time victory against Yugoslavia, in what was a rather different format than today with home and away legs for many rounds prior to the semi-finals. The USSR also got a walkover in the quarter-final against the most impressive team of round one, Spain. Some have reasoned that Spain's refusal to travel to the USSR was to do with Soviet 'support'[11] for the anti-Fascist Republic during the Spanish Civil War. However, it seems more likely that after a couple of impressive performances in early rounds (as we have come to expect from the Spaniards), Spain reasoned that they would f*** it up like always (as we have come to expect from the Spaniards), and just didn't fancy a trip somewhere cold where all the donkeys were either in the

11 Although the 'support' provided for the Republic was actually in the form of nicking Spanish gold and providing a paranoid Stalinist secret police and ineffective military structures. 'Support' in fact which was probably crucial to the victory of the other side!

Politburo or serving life-sentences in the Gulag and unavailable for post-siesta kickings. *[Editor's note: This casual and puerile stereotyping of our European cousins is regrettable but is alas typical of the type of thing we can expect from newspapers throughout the tournament, so we may as well let it slip through now to get you acclimatised: for, you, Tommy, the var ist just beginnink...]*

France were unable to prevent England's entry to the qualifying tournament four years later, but they were to find other and more devious ways, helped by jealous European neighbours, to prevent England victories. It is a story of the utmost importance and needs to be told[12] and sorry to say in 1964, it was the French who were at it again. In the first round home and away knockout the mighty, mighty England were drawn against our neighbours from across the channel (or 'La Minge' as I believe they prefer to call it). Not wanting to cause a diplomatic incident, and demonstrating our innate sense of superiority and fair-play, for the first leg on 3 October 1962 England fielded a team composed entirely of amateurs in their late 30s to ensure a French win and give the lads a bit of a challenge in Paris.

Alas, however, fitness told late in the game as England equalised and went to Paris without any kind of a deficit to make up at all. As a result of that, the team decided the best thing to do would be not to turn up until the second half of the away leg in February 1963, sending only a token presence of a goalkeeper for the first 45 minutes. This worked well with England 3-0 down at the break leaving something of a challenge for the out-field players.

12 Proof-reading services for the last sentence were contracted out to a small family firm in Tirana, Albania. They were cheap. The publishers accept no liability for any missing letters, like 'u' and 'n' before importance.

However, without the English sense of fair play, and with their man-to-man markers largely redundant against only a keeper (they used them mainly to keep an eye out for communists in their own ranks instead), the French also used the first half to bribe the referee who then sent off 10 English players for being late the moment they arrived. Realising the seriousness of the situation, the England goalie sprang into action, immediately pulling back two goals. In the end though, the strain of having to head down his own long balls took its toll; having almost equalised volleying his own corner against a post he was left hopelessly out of position as France scored on the breakaway. Adding another in similar circumstances, the French had won 5-2 (6-3 on aggregate) and England were out – victims (aren't we always?) of our own decency.

With home and away qualifiers until the semi-finals, the tournament itself consisted of semis and finals only, and was held in Spain, who qualified themselves, although only narrowly edging out Northern Ireland in round 2. France went out in the quarter-finals, losing to an impressive Hungarian team who, nonetheless, still lost against Spain in the semi-finals, albeit after extra time. In fact Spain were prepared to take on any communists you wanted on their own soil and after Hungary came a 2-1 final victory over those nasty Soviets – although General Franco taking a legitimate moral stance would have been as likely as, oh I don't know, say Alex Ferguson saying 'well played' after Manchester United have lost rather than whinging about grass length, shirt colour and the introduction of a new 'euro-second' which lasts 1% longer than the 'Imperial' seconds on his grandfather's wind-up stopwatch.

If all of this sounds rather absurd then of course it is, but then of course these are also the bizarre days when people didn't wash and took their holidays in Britain. In 1968, and after being trounced by Yugoslavia 6-2 on aggregate in the quarter-finals, the French lost interest in the tournament and in the end it was only fate that conspired against England rather than the French. First up was qualification, doubling as the Home Nations tournament. England lost at home to Scotland but still qualified with a draw at Hampden Park after beating Wales and Northern Ireland twice; that must have pissed the Scots off a lot, especially since Denis Law had described that moment in 1966 as the worst of his life![13] In the quarter-finals England beat holders Spain home and away proving again that we're the best team in the world.

The semi-finals were interesting; the hosts – Italy – drew 0-0 with the USSR. No, that wasn't the interesting bit...and they then won on the toss of a coin (and they say penalties are unfair?). In the third place game England proved themselves the best team of the tournament by beating the USSR 2-0 without the aid of a coin, but by then a freak 1-0 loss to Yugoslavia had seen the latter qualify for the final. Incidentally, although the final is of only incidental and minor interest because of England's absence, Italy won 2-0 after a replay – which prompts you to ask if someone had lost the 'special' coin normally reserved for Italian draws?

In 1972 England had only themselves to blame, as complacency rather than conspiracy ended our hopes. Despite top scoring at the group stage the assumption

---

13 He is reported to have walked off a golf course just in time to be told of England's extra-time triumph.

that two world wars and one World Cup would soon add a European Championship led to disaster with England bowing out to Germany 3-1 on aggregate (in the home and away knockout stage) with all the goals coming in the crucial first leg at Wembley. The English press had been remarkably cocky beforehand, but it would be almost 30 years before we could once again assume total superiority over the Germans. But at the time the manner of defeat and stylish superiority of the German football were no less devastating than England's more recent 5-1 win in Munich. Still, it must be added that at the finals Germany beat the hosts Belgium in the semi-finals, despite trailing, and then demolished the USSR (finalists for a third time) 3-0 to win the Championships.

England's Euro-failures were a source of amusement to our European neighbours but they rightly feared that sooner or later talent would win out, so in 1976 a complex formula was worked out to deny England victory. Well actually no, having started this history convinced that it must all be a plot against England, I must now admit that little evidence exists for that proposition, apart from my own insane mind and its continuing conviction, contrary to the evidence, that England ought really to be best. On the other hand, the history of the Championships can appear frustrating and at least suggest that it is all a plot against us. For the Yugoslav championships, for example, England started out with a crushing 3-0 victory over Czechoslovakia in qualifying, which isn't a bad result against two countries. And who then won the entire Championships? Czechoslovakia of course. Meanwhile, who scored more points than any other runner-up in the days before play-offs for runners-up? England. It just doesn't seem right and so even though I may not be able to substantiate the conspiracy argument in all respects, I am tempted to argue that it still exists!

There does seem to be something about the European Championships. It is almost like Scotland and the World Cup; we've beaten the right team at the wrong time and slipped up when it mattered most. But anyway, apart from England slaughtering the eventual winners and then not qualifying, 1976 did have much to commend it as a competition. Both semi-finals went to extra-time and both had goals. In the dual battles of bourgeois decadence versus communist steel it was one to each ideology with the Czechs and Slovaks seeing off the Orange Machine (*La Naranja Mecanica*) of Holland 3-1 and West Germany fighting back from 2-0 down at half time to beat hosts Yugoslavia 4-2 after extra time. Thus even though West Germany had already recovered from behind in 1972 to beat the hosts in the semi-final, Yugoslavia fell into the same trap. Whatever the Serbo-Croat for 'off the Germans' is, it was scribbled all over that changing room wall at half-time – and as ever, writing 'off the Germans' was not justified.

In the final, and although having a numerical advantage of two countries to a half, Czechoslovakia were clear underdogs. Despite this, only the usual German comeback forced the game into extra time at 2-2 before the Germans were beaten in a penalty shoot-out. Boy that feels good. Shall we do it again? Why not?! – 'before the Germans were beaten in a penalty shoot-out.' The decisive penalty was actually one of those cheeky ones that Lineker failed to bring off against Brazil but that Di Canio usually gets right. But even though they may have lost, it has to be admitted that the 1972 and 1976 European Championships, sandwiching the World Cup in Germany 1974, really and truly established Germany's supremacy over England and cemented their phenomenal reputation for tenacity and efficiency.

And sorry though it is to say they were at it again in 1980. 1980 was the first major tournament that England qualified for while I was old enough to remember it and so caused me particular pain. What a disappointment, although all I really remember was the constant talk of English hooligans. Having drawn with Belgium the English press had us down – in typical fashion – as the worst team ever, although this is once again an unnecessary belittling of Belgium (which is for the most part a fantastic, yet quirky, country) whose team then went on to reach the final by topping the group.

When I first thought that the 'conspiracy' theme might fit a history of the European Championships it was 1980 I was thinking of. I saw the group league table and it had seemed to me that Belgium and Italy had played out a 0-0 draw, rendering England's final game in group B against Spain irrelevant. However, on closer inspection, the top teams in each group contested the final (rather than qualifying for a Winner A v Runner Up B semi-final arrangement), so that Italy had actually needed to beat Belgium to reach the final. This makes England's draw against Belgium look somewhat respectable does it not, especially as Italy went on, two years later, to win the World Cup in Spain? In 1980 however, the 0-0 draw against Belgium only qualified Italy for the third place play-off where they won a 9-8 penalty shoot out against the Czechs.[14] As for England, they had not been robbed but merely unlucky, a draw against the finalists and a 1-0 defeat to the hosts hardly being disgraceful results.

England's qualifiers for 1980 were curious, as they headed the group from Northern Ireland, then Eire, then Bulgaria and finally the free-scoring but hard-losing Danes. Eire were the only team to take a point off England, who scored more goals than anyone else (22) and finished with a goal difference even better than West Germany who conceded only one goal – in a 5-1 rout of the Welsh. But as previously, England's qualifying supremacy – with a win percentage more than 10% better than anyone else in the competition – was not translated into final success.

Scotland's success in qualifying for World Cups was similarly not translated into European qualification. 1984 saw them win just one qualifying game – against East Germany. Meanwhile Wales didn't qualify in agonising fashion (surprise). After drawing a game at home to Yugoslavia which would have seen them qualify had they won, they would still have qualified if the Yugoslavs had failed to beat Bulgaria in the last group match. However, they won 3-2 to head Wales by a point and with the same goal difference. Northern Ireland, after their excellent World Cup in Spain in 1982 were even more unlucky not to make France 1984; having done the double over the real (West), otherwise undefeated, Germans they nonetheless lost out to them on goal difference, having lost in Turkey and Austria.

14 Odd, the Italians have a terrible penalty record; almost as bad as England. Except they beat the Czechs, who had beaten the Germans. But Italy have always been better at the flip-the-coin scenario.

As for England and 1984, well surely some kind of conspiracy theory is justified to explain what happened to Denmark. Bottom of a group including Northern Ireland in 1980, Denmark were transformed into table toppers in 1984, beating England at Wembley to head Group 3 by a point from England at the finish. Out of eight groups, England had the fourth best record but were eliminated by the team with the third best; only Holland were more harshly treated in having the second best playing record and being eliminated on goal average by the team with the best record, Spain. If that seems harsh why not add to the mix that Spain only had the same goal difference in the first place (thus causing the reversion to 'goal average' as a method of calculation) because they won the last game of the group 12-1 against Malta. If you add to this the fact that that game was played last after all the others had been completed, and that Spain (who doubled their tournament tally in this one game) had previously struggled to a 3-2 win in Malta and you begin to feel that maybe there is something in the conspiracy idea after all! Somewhat dully France won the final. I don't want to talk about that.

In recent years, England have established something of a reputation for getting results in important games to qualify for tournaments. Those with short memories will remember Turkey for this year's competition (2004). Beyond that was Beckham's last minute goal against Greece (2-2) and the 5-1 win in Germany to qualify for the 2002 World Cup. Before that still, a play-off win against Scotland and a 0-0 draw in Rome. Back further and vague memories of cold wet nights in Poland. Often, in fact, England appear to have produced something very special when it was needed. Back in 1988 qualifying, England needed to avoid defeat in Yugoslavia to qualify for the finals in West Germany. They not only did that, but turned in a towering display to finish 4-1.

Despite such heroics, and along the way the game which inspired the headline 'England Eight Turkey For Dinner', England's performance in the finals was, alas, woeful. True they did lose to the eventual winners (Holland 3-1) and the other finalists (USSR 3-1) but also lost to Ireland. Unless being rubbish and coming up against better teams can be regarded as a conspiracy, there was no conspiracy. England deserved to lose; the European Championship curse had struck again.

However, 1992 was a different kettle of fish. 1992 was of course a very important year for the 'European project' of integration. It was the year of the Single European Act (SEA) and a time when federalists dreamed of a more united and co-operative Europe. Only one thing stood in their way – the sceptics. Accordingly it was decided that the 1992 Championships should be won by a eurosceptic country. Knowing glances and significant nods were exchanged in corridors. Winks and grins passed between eurocrats the continent over, and mythical EMUs (as the Euro was tentatively – and much more amusingly – known then) were transferred furtively to Swiss bank accounts. It was all set for England to win (even if this story is one concocted by my own overly fertile imagination and even if Graham Taylor was the manager so that no one will ever believe it.)

But before that came qualifying. San Marino and the Faroes were added to the list of teams competing so that Malta, Cyprus, and Luxembourg no longer had need of feeling like the ultimate minnows. That said, although San Marino managed but a single goal, the Faroes actually won their first game (1-0 against Austria) and recovered from a goal down to take a point in Belfast. This put them well ahead of Cyprus, Luxembourg and Turkey who all got 'nil point'. What an improvement the Turks managed in 10 years!

England again needed something from their last game away to Poland and got it. Although trailing in the grim November weather, Lineker got a rare goal from distance (six yards) to ensure the crucial point. Scotland meanwhile also managed to qualify, heading a tight group with 11 points, from Switzerland and Romania (10) and Bulgaria (9). Northern Ireland were at least scoring the occasional goal in those days, although the home draw against the Faroes was indicative of their long-term decline. Wales – in similar fashion to Italy and the 2004 campaign – beat Germany at home, only to be thrashed 4-1 away. They finished – then as now – second in the group, but alas before the days of play-offs.

The finals were bizarre to say the least. San Marino playing in the qualifying tournament is one thing, but Denmark playing in the finals after Civil War saw Yugoslavia excluded is another. One minute the Danish players were lying on the beach and the next UEFA says 'fancy a kick about in Sweden?' And then the USSR, who had qualified, were suddenly replaced by an insurance company who were no match even for the Scots, who won the Group B wooden spoon match (Scotland 3-0 CIS). As for England, they were not destined to be the eurosceptics winners. Despite drawing against the ill-prepared Danes 0-0 and the French with the same score,

England were eliminated by hosts Sweden. The Danes – who also lost to Sweden – still managed to qualify from that group after beating France.

Oddly enough, teams who had won, drawn and lost at the group stage ended up contesting the final, whilst Holland and Sweden had to settle for semi-final defeat despite qualifying undefeated and impressively. So the final was between the arch 'Europeans', Germany (with their slogan 'we're all German now! Did we say German? Err, that's just our crazy sense of humour...we mean we're all European now...obviously, ho ho!') and the eurosceptical Danes. Much to everyone's joy the Germans were defeated, although alas they were not to offer such pleasure four years later in England.

Scots seem to me to look back on Euro 96 with some affection. The manner of England's exit – ruining the new lad party of Skinner and Baddiel (actually we can see how he'd get up yer nose!) – may have something to do with this. That said, England had a pretty good tournament and the manner with which they effected the Scots' own exit from the tournament provides some level of compensation in retrospect for the agonies of German penalty hell (again!). So with respect to those north of the border – nah nah nah nah nah!

Without England – qualifying as hosts – groups of five and six teams battled for qualification, with some second-placed teams qualifying as of right and others having to get through play-offs. With the 'CIS' and 'Yugoslavia' experiments having been abandoned a whole new range of countries emerged as the race to the bottom really hotted up. Cyprus were denied the wooden spoon in Group 2 by Armenia and only failed to finish even higher up by virtue of a worse goal difference than Macedonia (FYR to its friends).

Elsewhere, Estonia showed that half a century of Communism had done them no bloody good at all as they became the first country to lose 10 European qualifiers in the same tournament. On the other hand Lithuania – in the same group – finished a creditable third behind the Croats and Italians. Luxembourg were given the Maltese to boost their self-esteem, and not only did the double over their fellow minnows, but also beat the Czech Republic 1-0 just to show us they've been having us on all this time. Considering that the Czechs got to the final where the score after 90 minutes was 1-1, it just goes to show what a funny old game it really is! Getting into double figures (10 points) means that the mid-nineties are still referred to in Luxembourg as the 'golden age of not being laughed at by everyone quite so much'.

The Faroes were pleased to do the double over San Marino and Eire beat Northern Ireland to second place – by a whisker – to ensure a play-off place. The complicated play-off formula was calculated by taking the record of the second place team in each group against the teams which finished first, third and fourth to see which were the weakest two. These turned out to be Holland and Ireland. Holland won the play-off 2-0. (Oddly enough, against the group's top teams Northern Ireland had a better record than their southern neighbours, but their 4-0 trouncing in Dublin was enough to end their hopes...)

In the finals England peaked too soon – but deliciously nonetheless! After a 1-1 draw against the Swiss, the press and country were ready to hound and berate their heroes in customary fashion. However, the draw having pitched

England and Scotland to face each other, England's tournament turned around in a few short minutes. Although leading the Scots 1-0 England hardly looked convincing, and when – as in the first game against the Swiss – they gave away a penalty things did not look good. However, a fine save by 'Spunky' (still playing now in his 60s at Manchester City but then a spritely 50 something) was a prelude to a fine individual goal by Paul Gascoigne capped by an idiotic celebration. The rest, as they say, is history, although I'd better tell you just in case you didn't know.

The next game saw England play some of the finest football they have played. Needing a good performance and result England tore Holland apart. At 4-0 up and with the Scots leading against Switzerland it even looked at one stage as if England would win convincingly enough to allow the Scots through in second place. Tragically (and I use the word with not even a hint of seriousness) England took their foot off the pedal, the Dutch scored and the Scots were out, out, out! Shame. Also out were the Italians, who headed the Czechs on goal difference, but went out on the 'game between the two sides' rule (along with the back pass rule one of the more sensible changes of recent times). The general consensus was that Italy got complacent after winning their first game and paid the price.

The rest of the tournament was a case of the better side losing on penalties. England should have lost to Spain, but beat them on penalties. They then should have beaten Germany but lost on penalties. It was a similar tale for France; lucky to edge past Holland but then the better team against the Czechs who found themselves in the final after penalties, despite having lost to mighty Luxembourg in the qualifiers. Weird.

Of course you don't need or want me to go over the semi-final v Germany with all the stuff about posts being hit and Southgate missing in that hideous – why did they ever think people wanted football shirts as fashion items anyway? – grey strip. However, whilst England may have been unlucky on the pitch, there is surely some conspiracy in the fact that Terry Venables must have been the only person in the country who didn't think Matthew Le Tissier should have been playing.

I mean think about it. England play Brazil in a friendly and there are two banners in the away end suggesting that Brazil would find a place for Le Tissier. We qualified as hosts so there were plenty of friendlies to experiment with. And Matthew Le Tissier 'the undisputed King of Showboatin' according to Soccer AM, was single-handedly keeping Southampton in the Premiership. Matty takes the free kicks, Matty takes the corners, Matty takes (and doesn't miss) the penalties. Most of the team Le Tissier played with in 1994-96 went on to much lesser things (Craig Maskell, Neil Heaney for example) and yet Le Tissier was able to provide assists so un-missable and score goals so sublime that it kept that lot in the Premiership.

Major new research (to be published by Arcturus in 2004) suggests that Le Tissier's last minute change of mind about going to Spurs in 1991 when Venables was in charge may have something to do with it. Others have suggested to me that the fact that Venables is a complete t*** may have something to do with it as well, but that is a suggestion I would categorically reject. Still others might wonder how much cash other European countries stumped up to keep Le Tissier out of the team; although that is, of course, nowt but crazy conspiracy, it cannot be any crazier than wasting the talents of the most talented footballer of his generation and going out on penalties.

Did I mention Germany won the final? It was a so-called (how inappropriate) golden goal. I don't know if cameras exist which can prove this, but since I was there I can tell you that the linesman's flag went up before that winner went in (and I'm not making this bit up!). As the Germans performed the dangerous-looking, but obligatory in these situations, human pyramid of celebration with each arriving player flinging themselves onto the heap with some poor bugger at the bottom, the flag went down. Why? The Germans deserved to win, that much is true, but the last thing they wanted would have been a penalty shoot-out against the Czechs, especially after 1976 and the trend of 1996 for unjust penalty losses following unjust penalty wins. Did the linesman flag for off-side? Why did he change his mind? Was it simply so as not to cause a fuss! Oh well, same old Germans!

Euro 2000 was held in both Belgium and Holland. Although the tournament ended up in English disgrace, both for the ineptly led team and usual disappointing support, it is I think worth making the point that England's supporters behaved much worse in Belgium (famous for its stupidly strong ales) than they did in Holland (famous for its rather liberal regulations on soft drugs). But don't get me started on the evils of alcohol; that'd just be the hangover talking.

Of interest in the qualifiers was the much improved performance of the Slovenians and the appearance of Andorra, who couldn't quite match the depths set by Estonia (and in fact San Marino) for the previous tournament with a negative goal difference of a mere –25 for their 10 defeats (compared to –28 and –34). Two of England's three wins in qualifying came against Luxembourg, themselves still harking back wistfully to the time when they won three qualifiers (the spirit of 1996 and all that!) including 1-0 against eventual finalists. England's other win was 3-1 at home to Poland and so, by virtue of drawing almost all their other games, England sneaked through as a result of their head to head record with Poland. Even then, England's failure to win in Poland in their last game had left their fate out of their own hands. After a month's agonising wait they had the Swedes to thank for beating Poland even though they had already won the group. In a similar situation in 2004 Sweden lost 1-0 to Latvia, meaning that Latvia qualified for the play-offs instead of – guess who? – Poland.

After their flurry of goal-scoring activity in 1996 (two) San Marino reverted to their more normal number of one, which makes that goal after 30 seconds against England all the more remarkable. Liechtenstein also banged in a couple, needing both to overcome Azerbaijan 2-1. Malta meanwhile managed six goals, but no points, although almost upsetting Ireland who went to the play-offs and lost. As did Scotland, rather amusingly after winning at Wembley. Still, given what happened in the finals maybe they could have saved us the misery by having a sharper eye in front of goal?

Kevin Keegan's record as commentator ('only one team's going to win this now', etc.) is matched only by his record as manager. After the 'we don't know why but thankfully the Swedes have got it in for the Poles' qualifying campaign (the Swedes had also won in Poland!)

hopes were high that having got 'here', somehow things would turn out OK after all. In retrospect this is insane, and things were never going to turn out OK. Of course joy spread through the nation at a somewhat fortuitous 1-0 win against Germany, but by then a 2-0 lead had been turned into 3-2 defeat against Portugal. Keegan's famous, you-score-three-we'll-score-four tactic only really works a) if you have tactics b) if you actually score four instead of two. England were unable to muster either, and threw away another lead against Romania who as a result sneaked through after only collecting a point against Germany prior to that.

So, at least Germany didn't win and so little point in peddling any kind of 'Keegan planted by Germans after time in Hamburg' conspiracy. On the other hand, the French did win, consolidating their reputation after winning the 1998 World Cup, which they were so spectacularly to lose again after not managing so much as a goal in the 2002 World Cup – if I didn't mention it already, which I'm almost certain to have done somewhere in this book! In the final, France won in extra time against the impressive Italians, who won all three group games and the quarter-final against Romania relatively easily and then struggled to the final after Holland showed off their extremely amusing (but there's a time and place for everything boys!) comedy penalty routine.

That was a bit rough on the Dutch, who had beaten France at the group stage and thumped Yugoslavia 6-1 in the quarters. As for France themselves, apart from that defeat against Holland they also struggled against the Czechs and eased past Spain 2-1 in the quarters. In both the semi-final and final they needed extra time to win 2-

1 and again on each occasion with no little luck. The Portuguese golden generation were thwarted again. Despite the luck France had had, winning seemed to have become a habit.

Overall then England's appearances at the European Championships might not add up to the conspiracy I suggested at the start but there are certainly a lot of 'oh so nears' and 'if onlys' – enough to suggest that we may not have always had the rub of the green (although probably more than Scotland or Wales). Of course these days we've 'gone European'; we drive our Seats to the supermarket, pick up our pepperoni pizza and Stella, sit in front of our German TV and use our Finnish phone to call our mates. And Super Sven the Swede seems to have got England into the habit – with one notable exception – of finding a way to recover when losing, rather than looking hopelessly flummoxed and flinging high balls into the box a la Branfoot. So maybe this time, dare I say it, more than any other time, we are going to find a way, find a way to...well win actually. Let's all be insanely optimistic and believe that England will return from Portugal as winners for the first time of the European Football Championships, and not outplayed by foreign guile and tactics, nor kicked out in disgrace by UEFA.

History of the European Championships
Quick Quizzes

Historical Quiz 1

1 *How did England remain unbeaten in the 1960 European Championships but still fail to win it?*

2 How did Spain remain unbeaten in the 1960 European Championships but still fail to win it?

3 Apart from the fact that France lost, what else was good about the 1960 semi-final between France and Yugoslavia?

4 How did the USSR not lose the 1968 semi-final but still not make the final?

5 In the 1972 qualifying campaign, who got most points at the group stage – Finland, Norway, Malta, Republic of Ireland, Luxembourg or Albania?

Historical Quiz 2

1 Who scored the most goals in 1972 qualifying?

2 Who was the only team to beat Czechoslovakia in the tournament which culminated in their 1976 penalty victory over Germany?

3 Which was the only home nation's team to qualify for the quarter-finals in 1976?

4 In 1976 qualifying, which was the only Scandinavian nation not to finish bottom of their group?

5 True or False. Luxembourg produced their best ever qualifying campaign for 1976 drawing twice against Hungary and beating Austria to amass a mighty total of four points?

Historical Quiz 3

1 How many goals did Cyprus score in 1976 qualifying?

2 What was their best result?

3 In 1980 qualifying, how many points separated the group winners and bottom placed team in Group 6

4 Which were the two teams referred to above and what was the aggregate score of their two games?

5   *The highest score of 1980 qualifying was West Germany 8
Malta 0. But what was the score in Malta?*

6   *Who would have qualified for France 1984 instead of
Spain if the Spaniards had only won their final group
game against Malta 11-1, instead of 12-1.*

🏃 Historical Quiz 4

1   *Who had a 100% winning record in France 1984?*
2   *Which three teams have held the finals twice?*
3   *Which two teams which have held the tournament are
very unlikely to hold it again?*
4   *When was East Germany's last appearance in a European
Championship, 1988 or 1992?*
5   *Why was that?*

🏃 Historical Quiz 5

1   *The highest score of 1988 qualifying was England 8
Turkey 0. But what was the score in Turkey?*
2   *How many points did England drop in 1988 qualifying?*
3   *Why was 1988 qualifying group 6 not like the Eurovision
Song Contest?*
4   *In 1988 Luxembourg's one point from qualifying group 7
came against whom?*
5   *Did Scotland finish nearer the top or bottom of qualifying
group 7 in 1988?*

🏃 Historical Quiz 6

1   *Who had the worst finals records of 1988?*
2   *As in 1984, in 1992 Spain scored half their qualifying
goals in one game. True or False?*

3 Having shared joint worst record of the 1988 finals with England, Denmark went on to win 1992 despite initially failing to qualify. Did England fare any better too?

4 So who was worse than England in 1992?

5 The CI-who? Sounds like an insurance company to me.

6 Once all these post-Soviet types had gone their own way how well did they do? Azerbaijan for instance?

7 Wasn't this the glorious era of Luxembourgeois football?

Historical Quiz 7

1 In 1996 who finished bottom of Group 6 despite drawing away to the table-topping Germans?

2 In 1996 which two teams not previously in the tournament finished qualifying with 100% losing records?

3 From which finals group did both 1996 finalists come?

4 True or False? Over half the games at Euro 96 were 0-0 at half time?

5 How many games finished 0-0 at Euro 96?

6 Which two teams of Euro 96 were involved in more than one 0-0 draw?

Historical Quiz 8

1 Which teams (not winners Germany) finished the Euro 96 tournament undefeated except for penalty shoot-outs?

2 Of the teams which played in the finals of Euro 96, regardless of how many games they played, which conceded the fewest goals?

3 Who then was the only team to breach that impregnable Scottish defence? (This is a hint for anyone still grappling with the previous question)

4   *Who was the only finalist not to score at Euro 96?*

5   *Norway lost just once in Euro 2000 qualifying. When and against whom?*

6   *Which goal secured England's path to Euro 2000?*

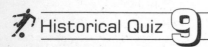 Historical Quiz 9

1   *Cypus finished Euro 2000 qualifying with a 50% won/lost record including winning their opening match. In doing so they were the only team to take points off the eventual group winners. Who did Cyprus beat and by what score?*

2   *What was the score when Spain met Cyprus in Spain?*

3   *In 1996 Azerbaijan got their first European Championship point against Poland. Did they get their first win in 2000 qualifying?*

4   *Azerbaijan's only other goal and point came, quite impressively, against whom?*

5   *Estonia got the hang of it a bit too. Where did they finish in Group 9?*

6   *In all the play-offs the teams were separated by a single goal at most, except for one pairing. Which one?*

7   *Only one team finished the 2000 finals with a worse record than Germany – who?*

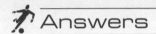
Answers

Historical Quiz 1
1: By not entering, despite what the conspiracy theory expounded in the preceding chapter!
2: After winning 7-2 on aggregate v Poland, they refused to travel to the USSR for the quarter-final
3: The score, 5-4
4: The game against Italy was decided by the toss of a coin – mind you, so often games are decided by tossers these days, eh Graham?
5: They all got one point each except Albania who managed a 3-0 win against Turkey for two points

Historical Quiz 2
1: England scored 15 in Group 3
2: England, who beat them 3-0 in Group 1's first qualifying match
3: Wales
4: Sweden, but only because they were in the same group as Norway, who did!
5: Like b******* did they, but they did do rather well in 1996 in beating one of the eventual finalists.

Historical Quiz 3
1: Nil
2: A 1-0 defeat by England
3: Only two
4: Greece finished top on seven points, with the USSR bottom on five. The aggregate score was USSR 2 Greece 1 with each side winning at home
5: Malta 0 West Germany 0
6: Holland

Historical Quiz 4
1: France who won five out of five
2: France in 1960 and 1984, Italy in 1968 and 1980 and Belgium 1972 and – with Holland – 2000
3: Yugoslavia, 1976 and West Germany, 1988 – they no longer exist as states.
4: 1988.
5: Because by 1992 stage 1 of German plans to dominate Europe were complete in the form of German Unification, 1991

Historical Quiz 5
1: Turkey 0 England 0
2: Just the one – against Turkey
3: Because although Cyprus got a point it was not from Greece, to whom they lost twice 4-2 at home and 3-1 in Greece
4: Scotland
5: Depends. They finished fourth of five teams, but were eight points ahead of last placed Luxembourg and only two adrift of the top team Ireland

Historical Quiz 6
1: England and Denmark both lost all their three games, scoring twice and conceding seven
2: Technically false. In 1984 they knocked in 12 against Malta to finish with 24 scored. In 1992 they beat Albania 9-0 and scored only 17 in total – so actually just over half.
3: Oh yes, Graham Taylor's finely honed machine were seventh best of the eight countries taking part
4: The CIS
5: The Commonwealth of Independent States was the name given to the loose association of post-Soviet states before they were quite confident enough to say 'actually we'd prefer our own country please, if you don't mind Boris?'
6: They scored their only point of 1996 qualifying in a 0-0 draw against Poland and also lost 10-0 to France. It is interesting that Cyprus got their only point in qualifying two tournaments earlier in a 0-0 draw with Poland. Well, when I say interesting...
7: Indeed it was. 1-0 wins against Malta (twice) and Czech Republic (who only lost in the final on a golden goal) as well as a 0-0 draw against Belarus saw Luxembourg achieve 10 whole points. Still nowhere near qualifying mind...

Historical Quiz 7
1: Wales
2: San Marino and Estonia
3: Germany and the Czech Republic were both in Group C
4: True, 16 of 31
5: Five
6: France and Holland, including one against each other

Historical Quiz 8
1: England, France and Spain
2: France, Spain and Scotland all conceded just two
3: England of course in the memorable 2-0 win at Wembley!

4: Turkey. Must be something about England, eh?
5: Their first game at home to Latvia
6: Henrik Larssen's goal against Poland probably had most to do with it

Historical Quiz 9
1: Spain 3-2
2: Spain won 8-0
3: Oh yes, they walloped Liechtenstein

4-0 at home. They did lose 2-1 away mind you
4: A 1-1 draw against Portugal, who avoided the play-offs by being best runner-up
5: Third behind Scotland and the Czech Republic
6: Denmark eased past Israel – oh yes, very European – 8-0 (5-0 away)
7: Denmark

UEFA EUROPEAN CHAMPIONSHIPS

2

PORTUGAL 2004

The Qualifying Campaign

It's amazing when looking back on a qualifying campaign that so many results and goals which seemedinsignificant at the time turn out to be highly relevant. Similarly, matches which seem to be important turn out not to be. For instance, England's home draw against Macedonia was thought to make direct qualification for England very difficult indeed, but although losing that game may have dented confidence, when looking at the final table, England could have afforded to have lost (even heavily) and still have won the group. Here then is the story of all the ups and downs on the way to Portugal

2004, including what turned out to be crucial in terms of how the teams that got there, got there!

Group 1

Could They Make it Any Easier for France?

No, not really. Whilst it has to be said that in recent years Cyprus have managed to put together the odd decent result (including a surprise 3-2 victory against Spain) and whilst Slovenia emerged as a pretty decent football team, this was never really going to test the French, notwithstanding their goal-shy World Cup and the fact that Israel had interfered with their plans in the past, not least in terms of the 1994 World Cup when the Bulgarians applied the coup de grace in Paris.[15]

But I digress. Actually, while I digress, I shall digress further. How do Israel get in Europe? Of course the answer is that they can't be trusted to play nicely with the other children in their own playground. Ooh I could go off on one about Israel. *[Editor's note: The subsequent 8000- word tirade by Dr Pettiford, railing against the global injustices of Bush's 'new world order' and Israel's place in it has had to be deleted. If you do happen to be interested in such observations, for a more balanced view we can do no better than direct you to another Arcturus publication* Terrorism: The New World War, *(2003) by, er, Lloyd Pettiford and David Harding].*

Apologies for the bit of politics. Anyway, this group never looked likely to test the French – that's the point– and with one non-European without a history of major competition success (Israel) and two islands (Cyprus and

15 Kostadinov in the last minute I think, but I never can remember!

Malta) for competition, it was perhaps the most pre-dictable of groups in terms of the runners-up spot too, which Slovenia took with some ease, building on their remarkable progress over a few short years. In 1998 World Cup qualifying the Slovenians had managed just one point from eight games, and yet in qualifying for Japan/Korea they went 12 games undefeated; winning five and drawing five in qualifying was enough to earn a play-off spot where they surprised many by beating Romania at home and drawing away to get through.

Looking at qualifying for this group it is difficult to find a surprise of any kind. France won all their games. Slovenia lost to France and were held to a draw in Israel but otherwise cruised into the play-off spot without ever looking – from the moment of their 5-0 defeat in France in October 2002 – like challenging for direct qualifica-tion. In fact what with having qualified as holders for the World Cup in 2002 (did I mention the fact that they failed to score so much as a goal in their defence of the title?) you could almost say it is a long long time since France had a genuinely competitive game!

The biggest win in the group was France's 6-0 demoli-tion of Malta, with six also being the highest game aggre-gate (in that game). The biggest away win was Malta 0-4 France. Unsurprisingly Malta finished bottom of the group, surprisingly earning their only point in a 2-2 draw away to Israel.

 Group 1 Quick Quiz (Answers on p. 77)

1 *In the year before the end of the qualifying tournament how many teams did France not beat?*

2   *Which tournament did France win in 2003?*

3   *Why was France's 1-0 win against Cameroon especially hollow?*

4   *At the time of writing (October 2003) who were the last team not to lose to France apart from the Czech Republic?*

5   *If France were so stunning in 2002/03 how come they were so, frankly, pathetic in defence of their world crown in 2002?*

6   *What was the difference in attendance between the final qualifying games on 11 October 2003?*

Group 2

The Luck of the Scandinavians

If Group 1 was Dullsville City, Arizona[16] then Group 2 was surprisingly close – and filled with surprises – with Denmark qualifying direct and the Norwegians some-how making the play-offs at the expense of the Romanians, Bosnians and Herzegovians (the last two playing as one). Romania, being the team who would sit out the final round of matches, needed to win in Denmark to guarantee a play-off spot and give themselves a genuine shot at automatic qualification. Deep into injury time they led 2-1. At about the same time Bosnia-Herzegovina were clinging tenaciously to a 1-0 lead in Luxembourg. Combined with their home win against Luxembourg, a 1-0 win against Norway in the previous game and a sur-prise 2-0 win in Denmark and that gave them a shot at – amazingly – winning the group if they could win their last game – at home to the very same Denmark.

Speak to your average Romanian on the subject of that

16 Copyright: that character in *Reginald Perrin*.

last game of theirs and one gets the impression that the similarities between the Danish and Swiss flags is enough to explain their elimination from Portugal 2004, the referee of that fateful game in Copenhagen being a certain Herr Maier from Switzerland. He had already awarded the Danes a penalty from which they took the lead in the first half, only to be pegged back by Mutu and Pancu in the second half. It is one of those games where the 'raw' statistic 'Laursen 90' hides so much. Herr Maier having signalled (a minimum of) four minutes of added time 'allowed' the Danes to equalise in the fifth minute. (Besides that game, the Romanians must be kicking themselves for allowing late goals to drop points both at home and away to Norway, and for collapsing when in control at home to Denmark).

Personally, I have little sympathy with the Romanians. For a start the whole 'added time' thing comes with a warning as clear as the ones about investments going up as well as down and about your house being taken away if you don't keep up repayments on a loan. There will be a minimum of so many minutes added time. Furthermore, if you want my opinion the Romanians are a bunch of diving cheats who were probably wasting so much time in the last few minutes that Herr Maier was fully justified in adding on the extra time. Although not based on actually having seen the match, this opinion is strictly impartial and based on the finest traditions of journalistic integrity. I am not swayed at all by having stood on an open terrace getting rained on heavily for three hours whilst watching the Romanian national tumbling team (aka Steaua Bucharest) dive and connive their way to a thoroughly unjust UEFA cup victory against the forces of truth and goodness embodied by Southampton FC. By the way, 'Steaua' rhymes with 'dour'. *[Editor's note: Again we have felt it necessary to remove another extensive tirade, entitled 'Why Does It Always Rain on Me?', this time against Romanian taxi drivers (b******!) and the inadequacy of the facilities at Steaua Stadium]*

So, the Danes' draw at home to Romania meant that they needed another away to Bosnia-Herzegovina to win the group, whilst the poor old Romanians were relying on Luxembourg (goals for: none, goals against: 20 in the first seven qualifiers) to nick a point in Norway if they were to have any chance. Their only hope perhaps lay in the fact that Norway – the team that was recently beating Brazil in the World Cup – were now absolutely sh*t and almost as shot-shy as the Greeks. *[Editor's note: See elsewhere for indignant tirade against Greek 'strikers']*

In the event it all still went to the wire. Denmark got the draw they needed in Bosnia, but no more than that. A goal for Bosnia would have seem them pip Denmark by a point leaving Denmark, Norway and Romania level on points. The Romanians still wouldn't have qualified, not in a month of injury time. But Bosnia did not get the goal in any case. Meanwhile, Norway won 1-0 at home to Luxembourg. This put them level on points with Romania and gave them a goal-difference of +4 compared to the Romanians' +12. However, the 1-0 win for Norway in Bucharest (83 minutes, bloody hell Stefan Iversen scored a goal!) coupled with a late equalising penalty in Oslo (Solskjaer, poor old Romanians) allowed the desperate Norwegians to scrape into the play-offs (of which more below).

The highest home win in the group was Romania's 4-0

win against Luxembourg. Romania's 7-0 win in Luxembourg was the highest away win. Seven goals was the joint highest aggregate for a match, with Luxembourg v Romania equalled by Romania 2-5 Denmark, a game in which Denmark were trailing 2-1 with around 35 minutes to go!

 Group 2 Quick Quiz

1   *True or False? Romania, who failed to qualify, scored more goals than both group winners Denmark and runners-up Norway.*

2   *Bottom team Luxembourg were one of three teams to not score in eight games. Who were the others?*

3   *True or False? Of the teams not scoring Luxembourg conceded fewest goals?*

4   *Which British-based player scored Norway's goal in their crucial 1-0 win versus Luxembourg?*

5   *In Norway's game against Luxembourg, who was the only member of the back four not based in England?*

6   *In January 2003 how many turned up to watch Oman versus Norway in a friendly?*

Group

Will Austria Ever Again Have a Football Team?

In some ways, the excitement never started in Group 3. The Czechs were a bit better than the Dutch. The Dutch were better than the Austrians, who were better than the Moldovans who outshone the Belarussians. In the end, the Czechs' 3-1 home win against Holland in September

2003 in Prague, enjoyed by fewer than go to Hull City home games, turned out to be the group decider, condemning *la naranja mecanica* (Spanish for bunch of infighting posers) of Holland to the play-offs where they didn't – *quelle surprise* (that's French for 'it's a fix') – get Turkey or Spain.

In fact the group might have been a good deal closer in normal circumstances but the Czechs performed beyond their and anybody else's expectations. After disappointing in the World Cup qualifiers for 2002, and trailing 1-0 at half time in Rotterdam, few would have predicted how easily they would control the group once the huge ungainly Koller had equalised in that match. True, even then the home win against Holland was eventually the only difference between the sides, but after an away win versus France in a friendly, the Czechs' confidence was sky high. They won the match against Holland 3-1, with Milan Baros settling nerves with a last-minute goal after the Czechs had led comfortably at the break.

Both Holland and the Czech Republic recorded 5-0 home wins over Moldova and Austria produced the same score against Belarus, whilst the highest away win was Holland's in Austria early in the campaign (3-0). The highest aggregate in a game was five, in the home victories noted above as well as in the Czechs' 3-2 win in Vienna.

🥅 **Group 3** Quick Quiz

1 *Wouldn't it have been simpler just to let the Czechs and Dutch play each other to see who qualified?*
2 *Against whom did Belarus' single win come?*
3 *Where did Belarus score their single away goal?*

4   *In this context, why was the only other goal managed by
     the Belarussians special?*

5   *Can't you think of any questions more interesting than this?*

6   *In the Czechs' final game, Koller's last-minute goal gave
     them a 3-2 win. What was the score when Austria's Schopp
     was sent off in the 63rd minute and why did this matter?*

Group 4

Oh Puskas, Wherefore Art Thou?

With the Latvian 'Michael Owen' aka the 'Little Latvian'
or 'Super Marian' Pahars injured for most of the qualifying matches, Latvia had to go through Euro-qualifying
with a collection of players of a roughly equivalent stan-
dard to – no offence – Grimsby Reserves. What a pleasant
surprise it must have been then to pip a Polish side who
qualified easily for the 2002 World Cup and a Hungarian
side with a great footballing tradition to a play-off place.
For the rest of us it was probably the surprise of the qualifiers, with Latvia languishing at around 70 in FIFA rankings. However, with the final group matches pairing
Hungary and Poland and leaving Latvia to travel to group
leaders and winners Sweden, things went right to a rather
nervous wire for the middle one of the Baltic Republics.

Poland must really be wondering about the Swedes!
The group looked to be between them and the Swedes
but after the first few matches they were already playing
catch up with a Latvian team that went to Warsaw and
won 1-0. True the Poles subsequently won 2-0 in Riga but
the slow-starting – then group-winning Swedes – had the
'casting vote'. Back in 1999 it was the Swedes who won
what for them was a dead match against Poland, which

meant that England qualified for the play-offs (which they won against Scotland). This time around, Poland might have expected that their last-day win in Hungary would put them level on points with Latvia and with a 2-1 aggregate win in head to head matches. But no, Latvia actually won in Sweden. Ultimately, Latvia took four points off Sweden whilst Poland got none (as was the case in 2000 qualifying).

San Marino was one of the teams which failed to score, and of those the one which conceded most goals. The highest home win in the group was 5-0 which both Poland and Sweden managed against the tiny Italian thing. The biggest away win was 6-0 by Sweden in San Marino, with six also being the highest aggregate score for a game. San Marino's best result was a 1-0 home defeat to the little Latvians, who many will feel were very lucky to have made the play-offs, although then again any team that beats Sweden must be pretty good; England never do it!

🏃 **Group 4** Quick Quiz

1 *True or False? Southampton would probably have beaten boring boring Arsenal in the 2003 FA Cup and even more dour Steaua Bucharest in the 2003 UEFA Cup if Marian Pahars had been fit.*

2 *Why were Latvia hanging on in their final group game away in Sweden?*

3 *Apart from group winners Sweden (+16), who had the best goal difference in the group?*

4 *Apart from the free-missing San Marino team, which team in the group found the net fewest times?*

5 Did Latvia get the round thing in the net more often at
   home or away?

6 Latvia got the most successful tournament in their history
   off to a great start by drawing 0-0 at home to Sweden.
   Only 8,500 saw the game. But by how much had crowds
   swelled by the time of their last home qualifier, a 3-1 and
   decisive thumping of the Hungarians?

Group 5

The League of Super Minnows

First they organise a special Korean World Cup to ensure
Germany qualify for the final and then they manage to
arrange a European qualifying group of various pathetic
minnow nations so that qualifying isn't too onerous a
task. Rumour has it that the German psyche was so pro-
foundly affected by the 5-1 rout by England that several
billion euros changed hands to ensure that if Germany
were to draw a home nation it would be a nice easy one
like Scotland. As an added precaution the Germans
decided to manage the Scottish team too. There is, of
course, absolutely no substance in any of the above,
which represents nothing more than a gratuitous excuse
to mention beating Germany 5-1 combined with unnecessary Anglo arrogance/anti-Scottishness. I should apologise for this, but decline to. *[Editor's note: This kind of
gibbering jingoistic nonsense is, as a general rule, deleted from
most books, especially football books, but if you take out his
anti-Israeli stuff and tirades against Bucharest taxi drivers , it
gets pretty hard to pad this thing out. Besides, he's cheap and
no one else offered to churn out 60,000 words in a fortnight. I
mean, how much did you pay for this? It's a bargain, really.]*

Theoretically, Iceland could have condemned Germany to a play-off spot by winning their final game in Germany. Was that ever going to happen? Even so, the Germans made hugely heavy weather of things up to that point. At home they defeated the Faroes 2-1 with the aid of a penalty. In the Faroes they didn't score until the 89th minute before winning 2-0. They also drew at home to Lithuania and away to Scotland and Iceland. But by the time the group was over, they had won five games and drawn three to qualify both undefeated and unimpressive.

Of those chasing second spot, the Lithuanians impressed except against Iceland to whom they managed to lose 3-0, twice. This left the way open for either Iceland if they won in Germany or Scotland failed to beat Lithuania, or to Scotland if they beat Lithuania. And, Lithuania being less formidable than the likes of Costa Rica, Iran or Peru (again, unnecessary and gratuitous) the Scots romped home 1-0 with a late goal and qualified for a play-off against the only team they ever got a decent result against, Holland. (For my predictable play-off predictions and whether they came true, see below!)

A statistic the Faroes would probably have settled for before qualifying is that the biggest win in the group – home or away – was 3-0 and didn't include the Faroes ('We're hard to beat' claims manager Henrik Larson – no, not that one). This was achieved at home by Germany against Iceland, and Iceland against Lithuania and away by Iceland against Lithuania. The highest aggregate score was a mere four goals, this number being racked up in three games; Faroes' draw against Scotland and two 3-1 victories against the Faroes (Scotland v Faroes and Faroes v Lithuania).

Group 5 Quick Quiz

1   *Despite a goal difference of only –11 in eight games, the*
    Faroe Islands only managed to pick up a single point in
    qualifying. Against which team?
2   *Given that San Marino, Northern Ireland and Luxembourg*
    failed to find the net at all in qualifying, what impressive
    percentage of games did the Faroes find the net in?
3   *Isn't that better than Scotland?*
4   *OK then, but it must be better than the others in the group?*
5   *Of the final group games, which drew the bigger crowd:*
    Germany v Iceland or Scotland v Lithuania?
6   *Berti Vogts?*

Group 6

It's a Funny Old Game

Spain (with Raul etc etc etc), Ukraine (Shevchenko etc),
Greece (the bloke that looks like George Clooney in
goal), Armenia, Northern Ireland. Pick two to qualify.
Simple, eh? Spain to win the group and Ukraine to go
into a play-off. Amongst the first two sets of matches,
now add the following results. Greece 0-2 Spain. Ukraine
2-0 Greece. At this point you're prepared to put your
house on either Spain or Ukraine and uninterested in
betting so much as sixpence on Greece to win the
group, or anything else, come to that. But incredibly this
is what happens, as George Cloonyadis and the boys win
six consecutive matches without conceding a goal.

True, the '1-0 with a penalty' win against Northern Ireland which clinched top spot didn't fill fellow qualifiers
with dread, but the crucial 1-0 home win against Ukraine

(Haristeas getting the winner in the last five minutes) was impressive, even if only 15,000 were there to be impressed. But perhaps most extraordinarily, just four days before that win, Greece had travelled to Zaragoza and sneaked another 1-0, stubbornly defending for the second half after Giannakopoulos (that's Bolton's Stelios to you and me) had given them the lead on the stroke of half time. David Coleman would say 'Er, quite extraordinary' and Dangermouse would say 'Good grief Penfold'. And you know what? They'd both be right.

At the other end of the table, and keeping up with the Luxembourgeois, Northern Ireland failed to score a goal. Twenty years after beating the host nation Spain in the World Cup – and notwithstanding a solid 0-0 at home to them this time which gave the group to Greece – it's been a steep decline for the team so proudly represented by stars such as George Best, Gerry Armstrong, Norman Whiteside and Iain Dowie [Iain, if you ever read this, that sentence surely merits a £500 donation to Shelter. I mean I know you and George have a lot in common but...]. Anyhoo, rumours that the country is to change its name to 'Northern Ireland Nil' have been slightly exaggerated – but only slightly.[17]

After their 0-0 draw in Belfast, Spain had to rely on Greece slipping up. Although this might have been expected, it didn't happen and Spain would have to rely on the play-offs if they wanted to make the short Iberian journey to the 2004 finals. The Ukraine, losing only twice and narrowly (away to Spain and Greece) paid the price of too many draws, surrendering a 2-0 lead away to

---

17 And it seems almost inevitable that their first competitive goal in a long time will come against England in the World Cup...

Armenia going into the last 20 minutes, a 1-0 lead going into the last 10 minutes against Spain and, probably most disappointingly, only drawing at home against Northern Ireland Nil. Apart from their point against Ukraine, Armenia – along with Greece – did the double over the Irish, er British, er Northern Irish. *[Editor's note: Another 30-page essay on the complexities of Irish history since 1344 was deleted here]*

And so Greece headed for Portugal, Spain to the play-offs, Armenia to the Black Sea (probably) and Northern Ireland back to the drawing board, hopefully with a big picture of a posty/cross-bar-ry/netty thing on it. It truly is a funny old game. Biggest home win in the group came as Spain beat both Northern Ireland and Armenia 3-0 and the biggest away win was Spain's 4-0 victory in Armenia. Highest aggregate was the match between Ukraine and Armenia. Armenia took a shock lead but went in at half time at 1-1. After half time they quickly regained the lead again only for Shevchenko to bang in a couple. Although the Armenians equalised almost immediately, Fedorov popped up in the last minute to give Ukraine a 4-3 victory. The kind of game the Greeks don't get involved in.

🏃 **Group 6** Quick Quiz

1 *Northern Ireland conceded eight goals in qualifying. 60% of all teams and 100% of teams in Group 10 conceded more. True or False?*
2 *Apart from France, did anyone in qualifying win more consecutive games than Greece?*
3 *True or false? All the group's 0-0 draws involved Northern Ireland Nil.*

4 *Who was the only team in the group to score more goals than it got points?*

5 *Which of Greece's players plays for the famous Aigaleo team?*

6 *That last question suggests I'm scraping around a bit for ideas and should probably take a rest?*

Group 7

You're Gonna Get Your F****** 'eads Kicked In

Well if this wasn't quite back to the 'Match of the 70s' in terms of hooliganism, it did seem – lovely Liechtenstein excepted – that this was the group of racist and/or violent fans. In this context, it is difficult to fathom how a small celebratory pitch invasion seems to be regarded in a worse light by UEFA than hurling bottles onto the pitch or incessant taunting of England's black players. National anthem booing is not in the same league. Clearly, England still have a hooligan problem, and with things under control at home it has to a certain extent been displaced abroad, where the lager is stronger and the licensing laws more liberal. But to some extent it is an issue of reputation. Ask anyone who has been to a match in Italy recently whether England has a hooligan problem! And in the UEFA Cup and Champions League Blackburn can travel to Turkey without problems, whilst a legion of riot police stood looking absolutely bewildered at the 2,500 smiling Southampton fans who reacted to defeat by Steaua with an intimidating round of applause for the home team.

As for the group itself, it looked like it was all going to

go horribly wrong at one point, but Sven's men – with the exception of one game against the world champions – always look capable of retrieving a situation. In both qualifiers against Slovakia they trailed 1-0 at half-time but won 2-1. At home to Macedonia they were losing twice in Southampton but salvaged a point; at the time this was regarded by some as a disaster but was ultimately enough. Away to Macedonia England also trailed at half time. Even Liechtenstein held England to 0-0 at half-time in England and restricted England to four goals in two matches. In fact England's ability to get the right result, and if not the best result, at least a result, from matches in which they struggled and trailed is quite remarkable.

Oddly, it was against Turkey that England seemed to have fewest problems. Despite not scoring until late, England's 2-0 win at home was a performance of pace and power, in stark contrast to the previous game in Liechtenstein. Away from home against the Turks, and without fans, England's performance was even more remarkable. England dominated. After David Beckham had taken his Jonny Wilkinson impression a step too far, hoofing the ball 40 yards over the bar from a penalty, and Scholes had missed an eminently presentable chance, it seemed England may have made the mistake of failing to score whilst on top. But as you might have expected the jitters to strike, and needing only a point, England remained steadfast and were able to celebrate alone in the stadium, joined by millions at home. The unbiased and hugely authoritative presence of referee Pierluigi Collina ensured that the 'crowd effect' was minimised in terms of outrageous home decisions.

With England and Turkey out front and playing last,

despite Sven's comeback kings keeping the nation on its toes, it always seemed that the real interest in the group would boil down to that one match. So it proved. One of the more amusing moments therefore from the many group games surrounded the playing of the national anthems against Liechtenstein, with both teams using the same 'tune'. Apparently this was rather less amusing when Eire had visited Liechtenstein as many in the crowd assumed that some terrible faux pas had been committed. So, England avoided a play-off against the mighty Latvians. The final league table includes little of interest, including the fact that Macedonia's record of five more goals than points is one of the highest in qualifying – equalled by France and bettered only by the Faroes (six) and poor old tumbling Romania (seven).

The highest home win in the group was Turkey's 5-0 win against Liechtenstein. The highest away win came in the return fixture with the Turks winning 3-0. The highest aggregate score for a game was five: the one referred to above, plus Turkey's exciting 3-2 home win against Macedonia in which the Macedonians led twice and at half time as against England.

🏃 **Group 7** Quick Quiz

1 *Which team in the group had the biggest d***head supporters?*

2 *In total, how many times did the Macedonian team manage to take the lead against England and Turkey?*

3 *How many points did Macedonia secure from its four games against the group's top two teams?*

4 *True or false? Macedonia have always finished fourth in their qualifying group for major tournaments.*

5 *Which game drew the bigger crowd, Liechtenstein v Turkey or Liechtenstein v England?*

6   *Do people ever make up statistics like crowds? (Inciden-*
    tally, recent surveys of the book-buying public suggest that
    47% will take this question seriously, 31% will not, and
    the remaining 40% won't give a damn)
7   *Strengthening the argument for greater Asian representa-*
    tion at the World Cup (not) which game did Liechtenstein
    manage to win in 2003 against a team represented in
    Japan/South Korea 2002 and how many people showed up
    to watch?

Group 8

Thank Goodness For The Beer

Talking of casual racism and stereotyping – as I was in
the last section – Belgium often gets a raw deal. But far
from being boring – as it is sometimes unfairly cast – it is
absolutely fascinating as Harry Pearson's book *Tall Man
in a Low Land* makes clear. Personally, I can never be
bored as long as someone is prepared to put a steak in
green pepper-cream sauce with chips and beer in front of
me, but as well as that many Belgian towns are rather
quaint and the beer comes in so many different types
and flavours it is bewildering. Even more bewildering is
the fact that so many English visitors do little more than
quaff too much Stella and say 'yuk, this beer's cloudy' or
words to that effect when given something else. So take
your holidays in Belgium. It's often weird but – if they
had hillsides – there'd be a welcome in them.

[Editor's note: Ahem...] Yes, OK, football...I was getting
there. After losing their opening game at home to Bulgaria, then unimpressively sneaking wins (1-0 away)

against Andorra and Estonia and losing 4-0 in Croatia, Belgium were always going to find things tough and indeed left themselves too much to do. Good job therefore that there's so much nice beer for them to drink as they miss out on Portugal 2004 (see, it was relevant!). A better second half of the campaign saw them narrowly miss out on a play-off spot to Croatia who qualified ahead of Belgium thanks largely to that 4-0 victory and a better head-to-head record.

The Bulgarians romped home in the end, conceding few goals and only succumbing to defeat once qualification was already assured. Estonian football – unlike that of their Latvian neighbours – hasn't quite got going. Perhaps they had a few too many Sakus post-Communism (now Saku is nice beer!) but two wins against Andorra and a couple of 0-0 draws were their only reward this time around.

The group's biggest home win was Croatia's 4-0 victory against the *rode duivels/diables rouges* of Belgium. Both Bulgaria and Croatia won 3-0 in Andorra and no one managed to beat four goals in a game, with Bulgaria and Belgium equalling that total set by Croatia-Belgium, but on this occasion in a 2-2 draw.

🏃 **Group 8** Quick Quiz

1   *Group 8 was the lowest scoring group. True or False?*
2   *Which group competed with Group 8 as the lowest scoring one?*
3   *Are Bulgarians interested in friendlies?*
4   *In what percentage of Group 8 matches did both teams score?*

5 Did Group 8 have the most 0-0 draws?

6 Where did Andorra score their only qualifying goal?

Group 9

Oh Noah! It's Happened Again...

What a start for the Welsh. Winning away to Finland and at home to Italy. Add to that a couple of wins against Azerbaijan, and Wales was getting distinctly excited about sport for the first time since egg-chasers supreme Gareth Edwards, Phil Bennett, JPR Williams and Willie John McBride.[18] However, Wales were unable to pick up a single point against Serbia and Montenegro and could only draw at home to Finland, in the end rather fortunately. Their chance to qualify as group winners was slipping agonizingly away. But it was the game away to Italy which really ended Welsh hopes.

At least for the first half and a bit, one could only assume that either God was Welsh (which would have been a bit of a shock for Christianity which has generally, not unreasonably, assumed him to be English) or that Paul Jones had erected some kind of force-field around his goal. Whichever explanation one chooses to accept, it all went horribly wrong in 10 second-half minutes when Filippo Inzaghi knocked in a hat-trick. Either God had nipped out to tend his leeks and daffs, or a power surge in the Romulan sector had seen force-fields affected across the galaxy. Either way, Del Piero added a penalty and one could sense further tears and play-off heartbreak for the Welsh.

The footballers formally known as Yugoslavia must

18 Willie John was of course Irish but people always like to look at books and point out the errors.

have been gutted, sick as parrots, etc. They drew twice against group winners Italy and beat play-off qualifiers Wales twice and yet still failed to progress! Amazingly, this is because in a show of 'we were all communists once' solidarity, they provided table-proppers Azerbaijan with all of their four points (as well as losing in Finland). Not only that, but at home Serbia and Montenegro were 2-0 up (drawing 2-2) and away they were winning 1-0 with five minutes to go and conceded two goals in five minutes. I mean Azerbaijan only scored one other goal (than their four v Serbia and Montenegro) in the whole qualifying campaign and that was in a 2-1 defeat at home to Finland! So you can go on all you like about a renaissance in Welsh football but really the former Yugoslavs just threw it away big time and should really have been in those play-offs.

As if to emphasise the above, the group's biggest home wins were Italy's and Wales' 4-0 victories over Azerbaijan together with Italy's 4-0 win against Wales. Away performances were less impressive with the biggest margin being 2-0 on four separate occasions. The highest aggregate score for a match was five when Serbia and Montenegro won in Cardiff 3-2 – not that it mattered of course.

🏃 **Group 9** Quick Quiz

1   *Which Group 9 team changed its name during qualifying?*
2   *Apart from Azerbaijan (twice) where did Finland's other win come?*
3   *What was the most impressive statistic about Wales' qualifying campaign in relation to the same statistic of any other team?*

4 *What, even better than Italy's, Germany's etc?*

5 *Do Azerbaijan ever beat anybody? (I mean notwithstand-ing buggering up Serbia and Montenegro's chances)*

6 *Wales managed it a few times, but when was the last time Scotland scored against the Finns?*

Group 10

Who Are Ya?

Much wailing and gnashing of teeth was effected by football pundits in the UK, who seem to have rather fallen into the trap of assuming the Republic of Ireland – or Eire – to be one of the home nations. The former management by Jack Charlton and the array of cockney accents in the team might have led you to this conclusion. However, in appointing an Irish manager or two and in toning down their success levels, Eire are doing their best to prove they're not England in disguise. (Ooh that sounds far too arrogant even for the tongue in cheek jingoism so far – sincere apologies, especially to Orla Benson, Allen White and that bloke I met in a pub in Liverpool when Saints drew 0-0 and 'if Heskey plays for England so can I'...)

This wasn't going to be Eire's qualifying tournament. Although Greece proved what might be achieved after a poor start, the away loss to Russia and home defeat by Switzerland in the first two games always suggested that these teams would head the group instead of the Irish. Despite recovering to give themselves a chance by the final game, it was one they were unable to take, losing in Switzerland who won the group. Russia, like Southampton in 2003 (he mentioned gratuitously), headed for the Millennium Stadium, Cardiff.

At the other end of the table Georgia struggled, but must have taken great pleasure in a 1-0 home win against Russia. Similarly Albania. A win in either game – or indeed a draw – would have given Russia the group and condemned Switzerland to the play-offs. Lots of strange results between these former communists; have you noticed?

The biggest home wins came for Russia, who beat group winners Switzerland and Georgia 4-1. Away results were less impressive with only two away wins of any kind. Switzerland's win in Dublin was crucial (2-1) and equalled in scoring terms the Irish's own win in Georgia (which was less so). The highest aggregate for a game was six in the opening match between Russia and the Irish Republic, which the home team won 4-2.

 Quick Quiz: Special Focus on Georgia

Apart from Stalin, having the same name as a US state, and a young, new pro-western president, Georgia has failed to grab enough attention in the past. We rectify that here with a very special feature which emerges, quite simply, as a result of getting bored with these quizzes.

1 *Dinamo Batumi is a football team in Georgia. True or False?*

2 *What about Torpedo Kutaisi, WIT Georgia and Zalaegerszeg then?*

3 *Is Temuri Ketsbaia, formerly of Newcastle, the most capped of current Georgian players?*

4 *Has Georgi Kinkladze scored more goals for Georgia than any other player in the current Georgian squad?*

5 *Who is the oldest player Georgia currently field?*
6 *What was Georgia's best win in the year after the World Cup?*

The Play-Offs

The satisfaction of playing appallingly and only winning one match except for Luxembourg, then relying on Sweden beating Poland (twice) and then losing 1-0 to Scotland and *still* qualifying for Euro 2000 cannot be denied. However, it was nice to avoid all that play-off business this time round, and watch the agonies of others from afar. Not least because this allowed the author the luxury of a whole extra month to write the book which was only ever going to be commissioned once England had qualified. Such are the harsh realities of the capitalist world that it was felt that you – the great 'British' public – would only buy this book in sufficient quantities if Eng-er-land had already qualified. Too right! So to the play-offs of which there were five for the remaining five places after an agonising wait (ha! ha!) of over a month for the fans of the countries involved.

Since this book was prepared ready for publication prior to Christmas 2003, as I write, the clocks have just gone back and it is 27 October 2003. Since all the following ties were played between 15 and 19 November I take the opportunity to predict the outcomes of the play-offs. You have only my word, of course, that I did not tinker with these predictions, but I hope that is enough for you.[19] My word is my bond. So, below, I suspect I will either be crowing about my fantastic predictions or feverishly explaining away their inaccuracy. This is the man who predicted Senegal as the shock of World Cup 2002, which should give you an idea of how seriously to take my predictions later on in the book.

Croatia v Slovenia: Winners Croatia

Prediction

The unpredictable Croats against the team that has become increasingly hard to beat. For Slovenia the unpredictable Zlatko Zahovic may well be the key. Imagine having the initials ZZ and still being only the second best player in the world to have them!

Prediction: Croatia 2-1 Slovenia and Slovenia 2-0 Croatia (in my extremely humble opinion, the most likely tie to result in a shock)

What really happened – first leg
Croatia 1–1 Slovenia (November 15)

Well, not spot on, but Croatia very much in the driving seat. Only the most extraordinary tip onto the post from goal scorer Dado Prso prevented the predicted result.

What really happened – second leg
Slovenia 0–1 Croatia (November 19)

Predicted as the one shock, ultimately I'm glad that the one shock wasn't this. Having negotiated play-offs in the last two tournaments, however, Slovenia must have thought they were going to do it. With the crucial away goal and still drawing 0-0 at home, Croatia had Tudor sent off after 58 minutes, leaving the Slovenians a little over half an hour to hold out. As it happens Prso scored

19 The fact I got them all wrong might also convince you!

for Croatia almost immediately. This left the Slovenians half an hour to save the game, which they failed to do and never looked like doing. Prediction very wrong, but this was always going to be tight.

Latvia v Turkey: Winners Latvia

Prediction

The best version of this story would involve Marian Pahars knocking in a couple of hat-tricks for Southampton before knocking in a third in three games for the Latvians. However the Latvians are probably wondering how they got this far and Southampton fans are wondering if they will ever see the great – though little – Latvian again. Won't be plain sailing for the Turks but almost.

Prediction: Latvia 0-1 Turkey and Turkey 2-0 Latvia

What really happened – first leg
Latvia 1–0 Turkey (November 15)

Well you never know, I might ultimately be right about Turkey qualifying, but far from plain sailing! Verpakovskis – who scored the winner – had already had an effort cleared off the line before his cool finish in the 29th minute. Turkey had a player sent off and in total have three now ineligible for the second leg.

What really happened – second leg
Turkey 2–2 Latvia (November 19)

Now this was the shock. Not predicted by me but welcome all the same! I have changed my best version to mean Pahars recovering fitness to partner Verpakovskis next summer, having led Southampton back to the Millennium Stadium and victory this time. But you know what I'm like with predictions! But beyond Latvia qualifying perhaps the biggest shock was the manner in which they did it. Leading 2-0 with 25 minutes to go, many would have assumed that Turkey would either play out time, or get the third which would have made them safe. However, that was not to be.

One of Turkey's suspendees was the goalkeeper Rustu. His replacement put a free-kick into his own net on 66 minutes. Even now one might have backed Turkey to go on and secure victory. But no, that man Verpakovskis – the new Marian Pahars? – outpaced the Turkish defence to equalise on the night. Turkey now needed two goals to qualify. It never looked likely. Can you imagine if England had lost in Turkey and then lost a play-off to Latvia having led with 25 minutes to go at home? No, neither can I! Maybe the fact that Latvia went into these play-offs unexpectedly after a morale-boosting win in Sweden and Turkey after the disappointment of again failing to score against England had something to do with it.

Russia v Wales: Winners Russia

Prediction

They really really thought they'd do it this time, and much as I would be delighted if they did, I fear any Welshman reading this will be thinking 'if only'.

Prediction: Russia 2-0 Wales and Wales 1-1 Russia

What really happened - first leg
Russia 0–0 Wales (November 15)

Well it wasn't just me. Peter Jones (on Radio 5) said

before the game that Wales would do well to hold it to 2-0 against a team which had notched an average of 3.75 goals a game at home in qualifying. But despite this excellent result, Wales are probably still underdogs.

What really happened – second leg
Wales 0–1 Russia (November 19)

It never really looked like it would happen for the Welsh and an early away goal dampened the spirits of the largest ever crowd for a football international at the Millennium Stadium at just over 73,000. When Wales needed luck they didn't get any. When they needed composure, they didn't get any. And when they needed to press forward and score, Russia just seemed to be controlling the game in cruise control. Not the correct scores, but the correct team at least.

Scotland v Holland: Winners Holland

Prediction

How did it come to this? There used to be Dalglish and Law and Hansen. There used to be influential players with European Cup Winners medals without Scottish caps (John McGovern) and now only players with FA Cup runners-up medals without Scottish caps (Paul Telfer). Alas, Scotland will be restricted to booing on England as usual, however much they lie back and think of Archie Gemmill.

Prediction: Scotland 1-2 Holland and Holland 1-1 Scotland

What really happened – first leg
Scotland 1–0 Holland (November 15)

Not as disastrously wrong a prediction as you would imagine! My 1-2 was predicated on an enterprising Scottish start. That they achieved. I then assumed the Dutch would storm back until the tie was safe and that Scotland might force a tense finish as the Dutch relaxed. All of this could still happen, although more of it might happen in Amsterdam than I had expected.

What really happened – second leg
Holland 6–0 Scotland (November 19)

No tense finish as Holland became the only play-off winners to play away first. Scotland failed to make this as close as I had suspected but surely no one actually expected them to do it? My prediction may have been wide of the mark (no one EVER predicts 6-0 unless they are eight years old or it's a game against San Marino) but I got the right team, and it was certainly much less silly than those who predicted Scottish glory and that Berti might actually be the right man for the job.

Spain v Norway: Winners Spain

Prediction

Sorry, Norwegians (not least 'cos they're all 6 foot 4 inches), but even including Latvia, Norway must be the poorest side in the play-offs. I could be wrong – and often am – but I predict an easy passage for Spain, before their usual pathetic capitulation in the finals!

Prediction: Spain 4-0 Norway and Norway 1-2 Spain

What really happened – first leg
Spain 2–1 Norway (November 15)

How is one to make reliable predictions if players like Stefan Iversen are going to score goals? Having given the Norwegians the lead, it then took Ruben Baraja's 85th minute effort to save the Spanish blushes, not to mention my own...I actually got one result (home win) correct, even if the score was hopelessly out. Spain, like Holland, Turkey and Russia, though must surely remain favourites? (My self-respect is on the line here!)

What really happened – second leg
Norway 0–3 Spain (November 19)

The Norwegian crowd must have been disappointed, but with the obvious exception of Claus Lundekvam (Norwegian Player of the Year 2003) the whole team has been disappointing. Playing against the highly ranked Spaniards, victory was always unlikely even after taking the lead in the first leg. The predicted aggregate of 6-1 turned out only to be 5-1 but the essential comfort of Spain's progress was even easier to predict than Holland's. The only people who must have been more disappointed than Norway were the Romanians, who would surely have been more of a match for Spain.

Conclusions

So, there you have it. In the end, shocks are few and far between. Most groups were won by the pre-tournament favourites (France, Denmark, Czech Republic, Sweden, Germany, England and Italy for instance) or where a favourite had been difficult to pick (Bulgaria and Switzerland). Where this conspicuously failed to happen – as in

Group 6 – Spain then cruised through the play-offs. Holland also got through the play-offs and Russia. Having absent teams like Eire, Belgium, Romania and Scotland are not huge surprises.

Finally, all the play-offs were won by the higher ranked team, except one. In that one, the 69th ranked Latvians came from behind to beat the team which finished third in the World Cup and which is ranked eighth in the FIFA world ranking. Yes, Latvia beat Turkey – the loveable team of Alpay, Sukur etc – and on what better note to finish this review of qualification?

Answers

Group 1

1: One. They lost to the Czech Republic 2-0 but won 15 other games
2: The Confederations Cup
3: The win, in the final of The Confederations Cup, came after Marc-Vivien Foe of the Cameroon had collapsed and died in the semi-final
4: Tunisia, who earned a 1-1 home draw in a friendly in August 2002
5: Who cares? Quite funny though
6: A lot. Cyprus v Slovenia attracting less than 2,500 and France v Israel over 57,000

Group 2

1: True. Romania's 21 topped Denmark's 15 and Norway's 9 and was almost as much as the two combined!
2: San Marino and Northern Ireland
3: False. Northern Ireland conceded only eight goals in fact
4: Tore Andre Flo
5: Basma of Rosenberg, who was joined by Santa Claus Lundekvam of the Super Saints, Henning Berg and John Arne Riise
6: A somewhat disappointing 500

Group 3

1: Yes, although the Czech coach was very keen to repeat the mantra about no easy games in international football after the opening game win in Moldova
2: Moldova 2-1 on 29 March 2003
3: Surprising no one I'm sure – Moldova
4: It came at home to the group-winning Czechs and took the lead in the 14th minute. A lead they held for over 20 minutes. Only a goal in the last five minutes from Vlad the Incapable – I mean Smicer – settled Czech nerves in a 3-1 win
5: No, it was a rather boring group
6: 1-0 to Austria and it didn't matter at all

Group 4

1: Almost certainly true according to any Saints fan
2: Not only were they facing the combined might of Michael and Anders Svensson, but also reduced to 10 men in the 73rd minute

3: Fourth placed Hungary with +6
4: Latvia
5: At home, thanks to getting three against both Hungary and San Marino
6: The crowd had, in fact, dwindled to 7,500

Group 5

1: Scotland
2: 75%
3: No, the Scots only failed to score in losing 1-0 in Lithuania
4: Yes. Apart from Germany who only failed to score in a 0-0 draw away to Iceland, Iceland failed to score on three occasions and Lithuania four compared to the Faroes two
5: By 50,780 to 50,343 slightly more people were in Hamburg than Glasgow
6: No

Group 6

1: True
2: No. England and the Czech Republic both managed five consecutively but Greece won their last six qualifiers
3: True. Three of them
4: Ukraine whose 11 goals earned only 10 points
5: Er, Anastasios Agritis whose one cap at the time of writing came against Cyprus in a friendly in front of 2000 people
6: Yes, but Greece really are a dull team so perhaps not all my fault

Group 7

1: This is difficult to say, but we should remember that England is easily 'up there' in any d***head table and beware of turning the whole argument into a rather essentialising, casual anti-Turk racism. Some of my best friends are Turkish. That said, what they have done to their Kurdish minority is disgraceful...[Editor's Notes: Despite the systematic murder and torture in 'Turkish' Kurdistan and the numerous judgements against the Turkish state on human rights issues by – for instance – the European Court of Human Rights, I'm afraid we had to cut him off again then. I mean he just goes on and on. This is a football book f'crissakes.]
2: Six
3: Just the one, at the St Mary's stadium, home of Southampton FC

4. True

5: According to the well known magazine World Soccer, both matches attracted 3,548 supporters. Maybe that's the capacity or someone just got lazy?

6: 76.89% of people do, yes

7: Liechtenstein beat Saudi Arabia 1-0 on 30 April 2003 with 1,200 in attendance

Group 8

1: True, with only 41 goals in 20 matches

2: Group 6, which managed 42 despite the group winners managing just eight and Northern Ireland getting none

3: No. Whilst 40,000+ turned up for their European qualifiers, including against Andorra, a friendly against Germany attracted just 10,000

4: Only 15%

5: No, that was Group 6, where the Northern Irish were involved in them all

6: In Sofia against group winners Bulgaria, producing a nervy last 10 minutes for the home side, who held on to win 2-1

Group 9

1: Serbia and Montenegro, who had previously been Yugoslavia

2: 3-0 at home to Serbia and Montenegro

3: Their crowds, regularly weighing in at 72,000 plus

4: Yes, Italy's biggest crowd was the 68,000 who turned up to see Wales. As for Germans and the rest, good but not that good!

5: Yes, Uzbekistan were soundly thrashed 2-0 in Baku in August 2002 for instance, but they did provide a rare moment of sporting success for Liechtenstein, who beat them 2-1 in 1997

6: For those racking their brains for the last Finland v Scotland fixture, the rather disappointing news is that the answer is 29 January 2003 when a player called Scotland scored for Trinidad and Tobago in a friendly which the Finns won 2-1

Group 10

1: Oh yes, very true

2: Again yes, they're all teams, although the latter is quite clearly Hungarian

3: No, some chap called Georgi Nemsadze has more

4: Oh no, Shota Arveladze and the afore mentioned Temuri Ketsbaia are battling it out to see who can get to 20 first. Kinky's not yet reached 10 for all his trickery

5: Temuri again, who's now 36 — assuming you read this in 2004 after March and they are still picking him

6: Their only win, but what a win, against the Russians

England's Journey

There is no doubt that England took huge strides under Sven Goran Eriksson. After Dietmar Hamann had depressingly scored the last ever goal at Wembley and Kevin Keegan admitted what the rest of us knew already, England's prospects of qualifying for Japan/Korea 2002 looked bleak. Howard Wilkinson's ability to get a 'nil' out of England as caretaker didn't help, although the 0-0 draw in Finland should have been a win – Ray Parlour's shot clearly crossing the line, before being disallowed.

When Sven took over for that campaign people talked of England restructuring, playing younger players and forgetting even the possibility of making the next World Cup. That we did was a combination of excellent football and the fact that Sven, unlike Wilkinson in that away leg against Finland, looked like a lucky manager. England were going behind and winning and getting goals when they needed them. Most spectacularly, in Germany Sven and his team gave England a result so good that no one had even dreamed of it.

In the finals themselves, was the luck used up with Ronaldinho's freak free-kick over an uncertain Seaman? Whatever, England had a great tournament even if one couldn't help feeling that with France mis-firing appallingly, we really had missed a chance. However, after the position when Sven took over, a quarter-final loss to the winners and the knocking out of pre-tournament joint favourites Argentina was certainly a good result.

What it meant, of course, is that expectations – forever high with the English national team – had been raised even further. We had lost to the winners. Beaten one of the favourites. In first-halves at least played excellent football. The losing (thankfully) finalists Germany had been absolutely stuffed in qualifying 5-1. We now looked to have a group of players in their late 20s and sometimes early 30s who looked like Portugal 2004 would be the ideal time for them to win something.

In the way stood – it seemed – Turkey, who emerged during the World Cup to be rather stronger challengers than English people might have supposed. Turkey got third place and suffered only narrow defeats (at group and semi- stages) to Brazil. This was not the team England used to dispatch 8-0. So expectations were high but qualification would not be easy; no-one wants to have to go through the play-offs and as Turkey who had to do that found out, anything can happen, including a side ranked 69 in the world beating a team that almost reached the World Cup final. Thankfully England sneaked it but it was story of twists, turns and drama. This match by match guide hopes to remind you of just some of it.

Slovakia 1 England 2
(Away – National Stadium, Bratislava)

With Sven's private life on the agenda more than football in the week leading up to the game, the England circus rolled into a very bleak Bratislava. It was raining and cold and a tricky first tie was assured. The pitch was as bumpy as the Slovak capital was bleak and England struggled to produce the football they know they can. Things looked ever bleaker (Sven must have wished he was home with Ulrika) when Middlesbrough's Nemeth gave the home side the lead. It was no more than the Slovaks deserved. England looked ragged, and their World Cup inability to produce in the second half gave little cause for optimism.

However, Sven must have said the right things at half time. England came out, sleeves rolled up and grafted. After 20 minutes they got a bit of luck and reward. Owen was the only one to react to Beckham's free kick and must have put the goalie off as he flicked his hair at it. As a striker Owen was forced to claim the credit although it was clear that he should not have and ultimately the goal went to Beckham. Nonetheless, Owen's contribution was vital. It was also much more tangible in the 82nd minute when he clearly did get his head to the ball and put England ahead.

England held on for three vital points in conditions which seemed to have little to do with international football. This impression was given further substance by the racist abuse which sections of the home support rained down on Emile Heskey and which saw UEFA take action against the Slovak FA. One way or another, England were just glad to have got out of town with what they came for. Four days later they were not so lucky.

England 2 Macedonia 2
(Home – St Mary's Stadium, Southampton)

The contrast in venue and atmosphere could not have been greater four days after the Slovakia game. As we know, Southampton fans are the finest and (according to a University[20] study) most tuneful in the land. Any right-wing urges were thus here channelled into versions of the national anthem. It always sounds a bit imperialistic to me, although the cricket Barmy Army's version (God Save YOUR Gracious Queen) to the Aussies has to be admired. In any case, the atmosphere was good as Southampton got the opportunity to host a full international for the first time in its new 32,000 stadium.

The pitch was also a stark contrast and could allow England no excuses. Not only was it immaculate, but St Mary's is the only completely flat pitch in the Premiership in the sense that its drainage system has no need of the usual slight camber. To describe the contrast between the pitch at Slovan's dilapidated stadium and that at St Mary's shiny new one would be to talk about the differ-

---

20 Editors' note: Although Dr Pettiford declines to state exactly which university, we have our suspicions...

ence between something very smooth and something very very rough indeed. Perhaps the difference between Kim Wilde then and Kim Wilde now would give you some idea of the contrast. Bratislava's was as rough as the proverbial badger's arse, St Mary's as smooth as an Armani suit.

At the time, the suggestion was that England's 2-2 was a disaster. As it turned out England might have lost 3-0 and still qualified had all other results stayed the same. We should not forget also that Macedonia took the lead in plenty of other games, including twice in Turkey for which they got pelted by bottles (seems worse than a celebration to me, UEFA?). The fact that the Turks squeaked a 3-2 win and England did not is largely a matter of luck. It is significant that English 'spies' watching Macedonia train on the St Mary's pitch saw lots of shooting practice and very little defending.

In any case, just as the commentator was talking about how the Macedonians would have been happy to go 10 minutes without conceding, they were even happier to be 1-0 up. Seaman, already in the nation's collective bad-book for what was effectively a poor cross from Ronald-inho, flapped at an admittedly vicious swinging corner and the ball flew in the top corner. England looked nerv-ous. Beckham, seeking an immediate way back on the pitch, hoofed the ball out of play, presumably trying to play in a striker who wasn't there.

But almost immediately it was Beckham who got Eng-land right back into it, bringing the ball down with what looked suspiciously like his arm and then floating a lob over a keeper caught out by his instant control. But Eng-land failed to relax and it was less than 10 minutes before

Macedonia had retaken the lead. Gerrard gave the ball away very carelessly in mid-field and as a poor cross came in Sol Campbell was only able to clear weakly to the edge of the penalty area from where a clinical side-foot shot was dispatched around Seaman again.

Before half-time England had their equaliser. Good work by Beckham to keep the ball in play eventually saw the ball fall to Gerrard, who was able to make amends for his earlier mistake by lashing home a half-volley after an excellent chest/thigh control. England went in at half-time in need of guidance from Sven and England fans hoped that the second-half World Cup malaise would not strike again. But strike it did.

In the second half play became increasingly compressed in the Macedonian half. Gerrard saw a delicate effort lob onto the roof of the net with the goalie in trouble. Jonathan Woodgate had a shot cleared off the line; surely had it fallen to a striker the defender on the line would have been avoided. Alan Smith, however, in for the injured Emile Heskey, didn't receive a chance of comparable ease, although of three half-chances falling his way a short-range falling volley went straight at the keeper when it could probably have gone anywhere.

In between those half-chances Smith displayed his youthful rashness as he got a yellow card for an impetuous lunge. Then as the match drew to a close a pointless tackle from behind when the ball was already out saw him yellow carded for the second time and hence sent off. I know the person likely to do an editing job on this is a Leeds fan so I'd just like to say that where Leeds fans see 'loyal' I see a 'liability'; where they see 'talented', I see 'tiresome'. That said I'd be quite happy for him to sign for Southampton *[Forget it – Ed.]* and in the context of this match his sending off meant nothing.

A late break by Macedonia finished in a weak shot, but as already pointed out, if all other results had been the same England could have afforded to have lost this one anyway. So often in sport the losing player or team concentrates on their own performance. While there will always be some truth in this, we must also recognise that it has something to do with the opposition. Sven was right when he said 'We should win games like this and I'm sorry we didn't', but Macedonia deserved their result and deserved their celebration. Along with Greece and Turkey they are the only teams to take points off England in qualifying tournaments and I hope with hindsight we can be as gracious about their efforts as the St Mary's crowd believe our Queen to be.

Intermission

In the gap between those two games the main talking points were the future of David Seaman, aged 39. He was not to finish the campaign. At the other end of the scale, Wayne Rooney was hardly heard of at the start of the campaign but very much a part of it by the end. Rooney's debut came in the friendly defeat by Australia. Many people were surprised by our defeat by Australia but not me; in a conversation with a Sydney taxi driver I had suggested a swap – a win at the SCG for England's cricket team in return for a win for the Socceroos in that one. It was agreed. He didn't care about the cricket as the Aussies were already 4-1 up and I don't care about friendlies.

Why should anyone care about friendlies? The constant encroachment by clubs on the legitimate demands of international football (although themselves legitimate when football has become such a business) mean that friendlies have to be experiments. Also I don't know if you have noticed but there are international teams which do seem to do OK in friendlies but never win tournaments – Colombia perhaps? If England turned it on and defended well in every friendly, every other team would have hours of video to look at to see how to beat us! So I am perfectly happy to see England swap and change in friendlies as long as we see the odd spark of inspiration and get the odd goal.

However, there is a theory of revolution which suggests that revolution happens not when people are at their most miserable and poor but when things have slightly improved for the better or when people can see some hope. Such was surely the case in Romania and other eastern bloc countries at the end of the 1980s. Interesting, by the way, that the west spent so much time protesting against communism and its 'elections' which allowed you to vote for only one candidate and now President Putin totally controls the media, openly talks of his disdain for genuine democracy and suspiciously arrests for corruption only those Russian billionaires who give money to the opposition...but then again Putin is open to foreign investment. That's by the by. My point was going to be related to how with football managers it can take only a slight downturn for their positions to look unsafe.

Perhaps the manner of England's exit from the World Cup didn't help. A freak goal and an inability – again in the second half – to create chances against 10 men. The nation, prepared for a party, got instead a rather resigned

Eriksson saying that we'd done pretty well. We had, and perhaps defeat to Brazil saved us from the agony of losing in the final to Germany! But it did seem we'd rather gone with a whimper; Lions in beating Argentina (which is worth mentioning again if you need to bring on the 'feel-good factor'), we were pussy-cats against their South American neighbours.

But in any case, that defeat to Brazil, an unconvincing start to Euro 2004 qualifying and then a 3-1 defeat in an unimportant game (one in which we made 11 half-time substitutions including hardly established stars such as Ledley King and Francis Jeffers) seemed to mean that a 'Sven out' campaign was gaining momentum. After the Liechtenstein game (described below) you felt England were just one defeat from saying goodbye to Sven. Surely this shows how much madness is around? This is the man who took us to the World Cup when the whole country had virtually given up on the idea! Those who play any sport themselves will know it is impossible always to perform at your best, but that the great players – at whatever level – are able to produce the goods when it matters. Remember that if England lose to France in the opening game of 2004. It is unlikely I'll grant you, but it is not beyond the realms of possibility for England to lose that game and go on to beat France in the final! In any case, that is the context for the next series of games.

Liechtenstein 0 England 2
(Away – Rheinparkstadion, Vaduz)

As with almost all England games of the current era this game was preceded by a story other than about the match itself. It might be Sven's private life, the night-club antics of a player, missed drugs tests or whatever. On this particular occasion – because the whole world hates us for a century or so of imperialism followed up by support for US imperialism – it was terrorist threats. Tiny Liechtenstein, unable to cope, drafted in police from neighbouring Switzerland!

On the pitch things were much less dramatic. England didn't win 7-0 so the press said they weren't good enough. The things they said ought to have pressured Sven although, of course, he didn't show it. A header by Owen and a free-kick off the post by Beckham were enough. A late flurry by Liechtenstein seemed to boost the impression that England had under-performed...but again one must consider the proximity of the Turkey game just four days away. After the draw against Macedonia it became a 'must win' game, and unlike the 'must win' variety like Liechtenstein away, a much more difficult one to actually win.

England 2 Turkey 0
(Home – Stadium of Light, Sunderland)

What's the difference between the Stadium of Light in Sunderland and the new Estadio da Luz built for the finals and final of Euro 2004? I suppose the technical answer is the difference in capacity and the language of the name (which means the same). There are also similarities like the great atmosphere they create when full. But the comedy answer – which you can work up into a joke should you so wish – is that you've got more chance of understanding the locals in Lisbon. Moving swiftly on!

Turkey had before this match – and of course pleasingly at the time of writing – never scored against England. But also before this match no one was assuming that this record could automatically be preserved. Sven (perhaps responding to pressure, however unlikely that may seem) threw in Rooney for his full debut. The lad did not disappoint. Alpay – not picked for Villa all season – threw out the message to Graham Taylor that in this game he would see the 'real Alpay'. If the real Alpay is a petulant tw*t then he did not disappoint.

The game started at pace. The Turks harried and irritated in response and Beckham was booked early for half an elbow which would keep him out of the next game at home to Slovakia. Then Gerrard did well to pull the ball back from the by-line. His high hanging cross was dropped by Rustu; Rooney's effort was well blocked and Beckham blasted wide with the goal at his mercy and in tap-in range. Thereafter Rustu makes amends; Rooney runs from the half-way line and clearly slides in Owen who seems to do nothing wrong but is thwarted by the keeper nonetheless.

England's chances are clear cut but few. In the second half quantity tends to increase at the expense of quality. Beckham's free-kick excites the crowd and worries the keeper as it slams into the side netting but never looked likely to have enough bend. Gerrard headed wide from a corner. A slight knock to Owen saw Vassell come on and look an instant threat, although he too is thwarted by Rustu. Another Beckham free-kick from Beckham is pushed wide. Vassell produced another save. It looked as though England might never score. Just 15 minutes remained.

And then Bridge (then a Saints player before being tempted by the dark side) put in a fine cross. Initially the great chance which falls to Ferdinand is pushed out by Rustu (again!) but this time the rebound is slotted home under the keeper by Darius Vassell. How UEFA take the same view of booing a national anthem and a pitch celebration as they have of other things such as racist chanting I have no idea. I wonder if they will be on hand as God Save the Queen is played in Cardiff?

In any case, Turkey finally emerged now needing a goal and in their only proper effort Nihat (player of the year in La Liga no less) must have thought he'd scored, only for David James to leap acrobatically to his right to tip it around. After that Kieron Dyer lost his footing, did well to win the ball back and then lost his footing again in the area. The referee, presumably trying to give the score a look which reflected the match a little more, pointed to the spot. Surprisingly the Turkish team didn't take it too well, but with the match already effectively won, Beckham blasted the ball into the corner for good measure.

England 2 Slovakia 1
(Home – Riverside, Middlesbrough)

After another 'doesn't really tell you much' friendly against Serbia and Montenegro, the pre-match build-up here was all about the England captain, who wasn't playing. Reports were linking Beckham – swanning around the States somewhere I believe – with a move to Spain. Fortunately, it was England captain for the day Michael Owen who grabbed all the post-match headlines on the occasion of his 50th cap, the youngest England player ever to achieve this milestone. Slovakia, needing to win to have any chance of qualifying for Euro 2004, were certainly in no mood to make things easy.

Despite this, Owen ought really to have scored for England after 60 seconds – the ball skimmed the goalie's thigh and went just wide for a corner. Thereafter the Slovaks were irresistible. They scored one (rather like Beckham's in Slovakia) and could have had at least two more in a first half that saw England in total disarray. So often in the World Cup England had failed to produce in the second half; now in qualifying they appeared to be doing the opposite and certainly needed to do the same again now. Sven didn't look worried. Well perhaps he did – a little!

Owen suggests that Sven put the team right at half time, telling them precisely what was going wrong and what they needed to do. Makes a change from previous managers. Can you imagine what Keegan said at half time in the last game at Wembley? Something like Mavis Riley – 'I don't really know Rita!' Anyway, it did look like Owen had been caught but with the ball possibly out of his control England can consider themselves a little fortunate to have got the penalty. But Owen made sure to take advantage of the luck.

Owen then scored a header from a fine cross from the lucky talisman Gerrard. Only a great save and the crossbar prevented Owen from getting his hat-trick. Meanwhile Slovakia looked beaten, paying for their profligacy when they could have had the match sown up in the first half. England however failed to finish them off. Hargreaves and Gerrard both missed good chances to make victory more secure but in the end 2-1 was – and had to be – good enough. Wins against Macedonia and Liecht-enstein would set up a final showdown in Istanbul with Turkey. But England had underestimated Macedonia once before – surely they would not do so again?

Macedonia 1 England 2
(Away – Gradski Stadium, Skopje)

Before travelling to Macedonia England trounced Croatia 3-1. Granted I have always said friendlies count for nothing but it would be nice if that could be repeated in the summer. Alas when it did come to the real thing again – and without travelling support – England did not start quickly like they had against Croatia. In fact, once again they had a poor first half, going behind in fact. Eriksson looked pretty close to annoyed. If he can only get the team to play for a whole match!

In a way the new 'better in the second half' system is an improvement, if slightly nerve-wracking. First Rooney slotted home coolly to become the youngest ever goal-scorer for England. Then John Terry was brought down – no doubt about this one being a penalty and Beckham took the kick. It is not a game which is likely to be remembered for much else. There was plenty of pre-game expectation in Macedonia, thanks largely to the 2-2 draw in England, but ultimately England got the three points they needed. Attention became more and more fixed on the Turkey v England fixture which would settle the group. Providing that is, England did the double over Liechtenstein. I'll put you out of your suspense...they did.

England 2 Liechtenstein 0
(Home – Old Trafford, Manchester)

Although victory duly arrived against Liechtenstein, nobody really expected to have to wait until the second half again for England to play. However, with Sven (and England) much maligned after Macedonia at home, now looking for an eighth consecutive win to break Sir Alf Ramsey's record as an England manager, the away side battled tenaciously in the first half. Perhaps the national anthems – the same tune, different words – confused the teams. Certainly it was Liechtenstein who attacked first, although thereafter they had to rely on some outstanding goal-keeping.

Beckham, who had received an outstanding reception on his return to Old Trafford after moving to Real Madrid, hit the bar. I seem to remember Beattie hitting the bar but I might be getting my games confused! In any case it was 0-0 at half time. However, within a minute of the re-start nerves were settled; an excellent cross and a trademark run and stooping header by Owen gave England the lead. Barely five minutes later a fine cross-field pass from Owen to Beckham, led to Beckham's cross picking out Gerrard. As Gerrard looked to nod it back, Rooney moved into space and was able to control and lash the ball home with glee.

England relaxed. Beckham and Gerrard were removed to ensure they did not get the yellow card which would keep them out of the Turkey game, which now was the main topic of conversation. But Liechtenstein continued to hustle, without, it must be said, much real threat. Frick's late run brought a smart save out of David James.

England's wins against Liechtenstein had not been pretty but, for instance, the Germans had gone much closer to failing to take maximum points off the Faroe Islands. It would have been a waste to produce your big performances on occasions like these. That's the sort of thing Spain do!

Turkey 0 England 0
(Away – Fenerbahce Stadium, Istanbul)

Before this one, England had won 11 of 13 qualifying matches under Sven. They had only lost competitively to the World Champions and had never conceded a goal to Turkey. Easy huh? Well no, not really: especially not when the only fans in the stadium for England were...well I'd better not tell you who they were, but where there's a will there's a way they say (although this 'way' required wit, intelligence and a command of foreign languages beyond that possessed by our hooligan element I suspect, so no problem).

In any case, the pre-match build-up had been all about Rio Ferdinand and his missed drugs test rather than the match. This seemed to unite the players in some sense of misguided loyalty. I mean everyone knows how important these doping tests are; you don't just 'forget' and if you do you should expect to face the consequences. In the event, John Terry deputised so well that Rio may struggle to get his place back.

In the game, Rooney almost opened the scoring, breaking through only to push his lob over an advancing Rustu but onto the roof of the net. Turkey however look a much more serious attacking proposition than the team which almost left Sunderland with a point. Even so, it was still England who looked the more threatening and it wasn't a surprise when Gerrard went down in the area and England earned a penalty. It looked fairly clear-cut but then again a referee less strong than Pierluigi Collina might have waved it away. His presence – as much as that of any referee could – reassured the millions watching at home on TV. Graham Poll, to take pick an English ref at random – would probably have booked Gerrard. He doesn't support Spurs by the way; simply any team playing against whoever I'm supporting!

Of course you are probably aware that Beckham set a new English record (originally set by Chris Waddle in 1990) for the biggest distance ever by which to miss a penalty kick, as he thrashed it a full 40 yards over the bar. A case of 'anything Jonny can do…' perhaps?. (Seriously, though, will you worry next time Becks steps up to take a penalty? Me neither.) Alpay of course ensured that the watching Graham Taylor saw the real Alpay. But still England pressed. Scholes tried to finish good work by Rooney, although as he shot narrowly wide many wished he'd left it to the youngster.

However, despite the fact England were playing well, and playing well in the first half, the longer it went on the more worried one became that England would ultimately pay for that penalty miss or that Collina would get one wrong. In a sense he did, not booking Suker (what a nice man) after a blatant dive in the area, but he at least did not award a penalty. Then Beckham does have the ball in the net, although it is disallowed for offside. Minutes later Dyer appears to be clean through; although Rustu spots the danger and rushes out to arrive at roughly the same time as Dyer, with a head-height challenge reminiscent of Harald Schumacher's infamous flattening of France's Battiston (was it?) in 1982 (was it?). However, Rustu's attempt to make what Tahar El Khalej did to Dyer look like a cuddle came to nothing, and the keeper himself was fortunate to escape with a yellow card.

With seconds remaining we get a picture of the innocence of youth. With Turkey pressing and the score at 0-0, Wayne Rooney is smiling a smile which will be echoed in many living rooms up and down the country, but only in a few minutes' time. At the death, a Nihat shot appears to be arrowing towards the top corner. It also appears to me to have taken the slightest of touches off Sol Campbell – enough to take it the wrong side of the post. The referee fails to give a corner and – for the benefit of viewers at home – England are able to celebrate on the pitch. Under Sven England have only rarely been pretty, but almost always effective. Subsequent friendly defeat against Denmark should, by now, not be fooling anyone. It's now time to see how we get on in the company of many of the top-ranked teams in the world; they will be fearing us at least as much as we fear them.

The Finalists

This section analyses the recent form, history and team selection of the 16 finalists, with some predictions included. In the conclusion, more specific predictions – based on the draw for the finals – will be made, so apologies if here I end up claiming that four teams will reach the final! Before moving on to look at the specific strengths of teams, and then in the next chapter particular players, it is worth looking at those not always accurate, but at least vaguely indicative, FIFA world rankings.

This, below, is a league table of the 16 qualifiers for Portugal 2004 and the five defeated play-off teams according to their FIFA World Ranking at the time of the end of the qualifying campaign. The number in brackets equals the FIFA world ranking.[21] Brazil were ranked first. Of course

---

21 These rankings have thrown up some bizarre anomalies and given undue weight to some really unimportant matches, but they are – nonetheless – there or thereabouts.

league tables are not always a good guide (Southampton 6 Man Utd 3 would be an example of where this is so) but for anyone outside the top 10 of this list to win would be a real shock and anyone outside the top six – with the possible exception of Portugal – a real surprise.

FIFA Official World Rankings
31 October 2003
[Teams eliminated in the play-offs are in square brackets]

1	France (2)
2	Spain (3)
3	Holland (5)
4	England (6)
5	Germany (7)
6	Italy (8=)
7	[Turkey (8=)]
8	Czech Republic (11)
9	Denmark (14)
10	Portugal (17)
11	Sweden (18)
12	Croatia (19)
13	Greece (26=)
14	Russia (28)
15	[Slovenia (29)]
16	[Norway (37)]
17	Bulgaria (39)
18	Switzerland (43)
19	[Scotland (58)]
20	[Wales (59)]
21	Latvia (69=)

Perspective

And this is a list of the European countries (and Israel who are in the qualifiers!) who, though they did not qualify for the play-offs or finals, are – according to FIFA – ranked above at least one of the 2004 finalists, i.e. Latvia down at number 69.

1   Republic of Ireland (15)
2   Belgium (16)
3   Romania (21)
4   Poland (26=)
5   Serbia and Montenegro (32)
6   Finland (41)
7   Israel (47)
8   Slovakia (49)
9   Ukraine (51)
10 Bosnia-Herzegovina (53)
11 Iceland (55)
12 Austria (62)
13 Hungary (67)

Other facts that may be of interest you before we look at the qualifiers in detail are:

Global cries for a merging of the home nations can only be strengthened by the news that only England – of the four – are ranked above Cuba (57).

Latvia's 69th place is shared with Burkina Faso.

England's opponents in the 2-2 qualifying draw at St Mary's (Macedonia) are ranked 91st equal with Albania, a full 85 places behind England.

With 204 teams in FIFA's rankings (propped up by

Montserrat), Northern Ireland's 118th place means there are now only 85 teams actually worse than them in the first place. If they still haven't scored by the time you read this, expect a hastily-arranged friendly against Montserrat. But they must have scored by now...surely?)

The team Scotland huffed and puffed against to secure a play-off birth, Lithuania, are ranked 97th, amazingly nearly 40 places behind Scotland. Mind you, they did draw 1-1 in Germany, ranked 90 places above them too.

The Hosts

Portugal

In the immensely authoritative *Arcturus World Cup: Fact and Quiz Book* (2002), David Harding waxes lyrical: 'You can just picture it already: Alan Hansen and Mark Lawrensen talking inanely on a brightly coloured sofa discussing "dark horses" for the tournament. As quick as a Jamie Carragher-thrown coin into the crowd these two pundits look at each other and whisper "Portugal".' And nothing has really changed, except you might want to add something more topical than a Carragher coin throw. As quick as a Souness temper and hastily drawn conclusion perhaps? But unlike the 2002 World Cup – when clever-clogs Harding was able to predict a win for a team *speaking* Portuguese – this time surely they do have a chance as hosts, and probably as more than dark horses. Despite that, and especially as their neighbours Spain failed so badly when hosting the World Cup in 1982, there is less confidence, or even blind optimism, and more 'surely we've got to have a good tournament sometime haven't we?' about 2004.

For many years the talk has been of the 'golden generation' fulfilling their potential. Portugal won the World Youth Cup of 1989 and 1991 and as many talented young players became available for the national team over the next few years it was expected that Portugal would improve upon their pitiful international record. In the sense that Japan/South Korea was only Portugal's third World Cup finals they did – indeed – improve, but that tournament was the end of the peak of the 'golden generation' who never, alas, became the 'goal-den' generation. Faced with a group made up of the hardly inspiring but efficient US team, the 'impressive in qualifying' Poles and the eager – but surely lacking – Koreans, the Portuguese probably felt that Poland were the team to beat. However, they weren't, and after crashing 3-2 to the USA in a thrilling first game, Portugal reverted to being dark cart horses of the tournament, eliminated via their own appallingly negative tactics – and perhaps a little bad luck – in defeat to South Korea. All that from a team ranked fourth before the tournament. The 4-0 thrashing of the even more disappointing Poles when it came, emphasized the wasted potential but mattered not.

Expectations then of the 'golden generation' may have receded, but expectation will still be very high because of playing at home. The occasional appearance of Luis Boa Morte in the team will not impress Southampton supporters – whatever his efforts at Fulham – but the Portuguese have many other good young players, including Luis Figo, who despite looking craggy and ancient will still be only 31 by the time of the finals. Others to look for are Fernando 'get yer 'air cut son' Couto, Sergio Conceicao and Pedro Pauleta.

Pauleta scored one of the goals as Portugal beat world champions Brazil 2-1 in a friendly in March 2003. This win can be added to others against Scotland, Bolivia, Macedonia and away in Sweden. In fact, of a dozen friendlies played whilst others were going about the business of qualifying, the only one Portugal lost was away to Italy 1-0. One thing which may not stand them in good stead is that – with the exception of the Brazil game – home fixtures have drawn pitifully small crowds. I mean surely the free-flowing and inspirational Scots deserved more than 8000? And although crowds for the final will clearly be higher, one wonders if such fans are likely to back the home team no matter what, or if they will turn on them as quickly as David Pleat on Glen Hoddle.[22]

Prediction

Host nations do not win major tournaments as often as you would think. Neither Belgium nor Holland won in 2000, with Belgium actually eliminated at the group stage despite playing more attractively than anyone in Belgium can ever remember. England fell at the semi-final stage in England in 1996 as did the Swedes themselves, at home in 1992, and West Germany back in 1988, so that one has to go back to France 1984 to find a home winner. On the other hand there have been a lot of semi-finalists, including 2000 where co-hosts Holland reached that stage. And Portugal are a talented team. Even Mexico as World Cup host nation has reached the quarter-finals in both 1970 and 1986.

22 This comment refers to complaints by Hoddle (after he had been sacked by Spurs) that Pleat had undermined his position with criticism. Since Hoddle had been sacked after seeing his team comprehensively thrashed at home by Southampton others might consider the criticism somewhat justified. Since Hoddle had previously left the Saints after they gave him the chance to re-launch his career, still others who believe in that sort of thing, might consider it judgement.

All in all however, Portugal do not have a winning 'mindset'; others like France do; Germany always make the best of what they have; England have lost only one competitive fixture under Sven (admittedly to Portuguese speakers). In other words, it would be a big surprise if Portugal did not get beyond the initial group stage but an even bigger one, despite home advantage, if they actually won.

Semi-finalists.

 Portugal Quick Quiz

1 *Before hosting this year's tournament, Portugal had qualified for more World Cups than European Championships. True or False?*

2 *Tottenham Hotspur superstar Helder Postiga (things will need to have changed by the time of publication of course for that phrase to sound OK) scored twice in his first full match for Portugal after a couple of sub-appearances. Who was the match against?*

3 *Somewhat bizarrely,[23] the sentence 'Liar liar my a-knobs on a-fire' contains the names of two Swiss referees who refereed consecutive games of Portugal in April 2003. True or false?*

4 *True or false? The Norwegian referee of Portugal's friendly in England in Sept 2002 was called Odd Bent Ovrebo?*

5 *Fulham's – and former Southampton player – Luis Boa Morte has been capped at international level about as often as Matthew Le Tissier. True or false?*

6 *Which two Portuguese players will be hoping to reach, or to have just reached, 100 caps by the time of the finals?*

23 Perhaps as bizarrely as me thinking of this question!

Always look on the bright side of life

Denmark

Just over 20 years ago the Danes, in footballing terms, were hardly even regarded as highly as, say, Finland are today. They finished bottom of qualifying group 1 for Italy 1980, behind Bulgaria, Eire, Northern Ireland and England. And yet, four years later, in a group with England again they won at Wembley and pipped England by a point to qualification. Perhaps amazed by it all, Danish fans decided to regard success as an excuse to party, and with their flag the opposite of England's (white cross, red background) have become a mirror image of England in so many respects, both on, but more especially off, the pitch.

Historically expectations of the Danish team are low, and so success is relatively easy to achieve in this context. The fans are male and female and about as intimidating as a very fluffy bunny rabbit on a very fluffy (possibly pink or pale yellow) pillow, although considerably noisier, it must be admitted. Rumour has it, in fact, that if you play 'God Save the Queen' backwards it is actually 'Let's all have a disco' in Danish. Hanging on for a draw in Bosnia to qualify for 2004 was not too inspiring, but the Danes proved themselves a decent side by winning at Old Trafford in a post-qualification friendly in a rare defeat for Sven's men.

But back in 1992 Denmark produced the most remarkable performance in European Championship history. Failing to qualify for the tournament in neighbouring Sweden was presumably a disappointment to players and fans alike, but also – one suspects – something which was kept very much in perspective too. However, with Yugoslavia ousted from the tournament for political reasons, in stepped the Danes; returning at short notice from the beaches of southern France and wherever else, the Danes made a mockery of the idea of preparation, playing fantastic – and steadily improving – football ultimately to overcome the (it was them again) Germans in the final.

Denmark's team today has some familiar faces and – unlike the days when England losing to Denmark would have been a big shock – these days it is a bit like, say, Charlton winning against Liverpool. You feel that England/Liverpool should win, but then again you have to confess that Charlton/Denmark have got some good players whose teamwork might just swing it. Fortunately, and despite the friendly game in November 2003, such was not the case in Japan as England eased home 3-0 in the rain – but it could have been.

Talking of Charlton, one of the best known names in the Danish team – at least in England – would be Claus Jensen, along with Niklas Jensen of Manchester City. In goal they have Thomas Sorensen, lucky not to be credited with Rio Ferdinand's World Cup goal. Thomas 'is it Lee Carsley?' Gravesen of Everton and Jesper 'I'm afraid we can afford better players than you now' Gronkjaer of Chelsea will also feature. Newcastle fans will remember with a grimace Jon Dahl Tomasson, although he has fared much better in Italy. Per Frandsen of Bolton doesn't get much of a look-in these days. Peter Lovenkrands looks pretty good against the likes of Motherwell and Partick Thistle.

Quite a few Danes play, like Tomasson, in Italy, including Helveg and Laursen, and in other European countries too. Sharing the goal-scoring duties with Tomasson will be Dennis Rommedahl who plays in Holland and Ebbe Sand who plays for Schalke 04 in Germany. Poulson is also at Schalke. There are a couple of Danes playing for Panathinaikos as well as several still playing for FC Copenhagen, Brondby, Odense or Aalborg. Peter Skov-Jensen plays for the superbly named Midtjylland...who are ya?

Prediction

After surprising the football world by qualifying at England's expense back in 1984, Denmark's record in European Championships has been remarkable. They were actually the worst team at the finals in 1988 and 2000 and were disappointing in 1996, and yet in the only tournament they didn't qualify for, they were invited as guests and romped home by beating Germany in the final – and not just the shadow of a Germany we see over 10 years later but the World Cup holders. In *The World Cup Fact and Quiz Book* (Arcturus, 2002) I confidently predicted that the USA had no chance by using the words 'zip, zero, zilch, nada'. But some inspired play and being in the 'reserves' half of the draw meant that they were actually quarter-finalists. So, whilst I would be very surprised by Danish success, neither is it something I would rule out. About the same level of probability as Southampton getting to an FA Cup final.

Eliminated at group stage, subject to the 'Carlsberg Clause' (i.e. probably)

Denmark Quick Quiz

1 *How many games in a row did Denmark win before drawing against Romania at home in European qualifying?*
2 *In that draw, when did the Danes equalise, in effect smoothing their path to European qualification?*
3 *Does Stig Tofting, half-man, half-Rottweiler, still play for Denmark?*
4 *Are all Danish midfielders required to shave their heads as part of some crazy Viking ritual?*
5 *Denmark qualified for Euro 2004 after securing a vital 1-1 draw away to the footballers formerly known as parts of Yugoslavia. But who scored for the Danes in the home match against the very same Bosnians and Herzegovinians?*
6 *Which famous former player currently coaches Denmark?*

Rubbish, but don't write us off

Germany

Absolutely typical I guess. Germany were playing away to the Faroe Islands in qualifying and were drawing 0-0. The added time board was being adjusted and the locals were beginning to nudge each other nervously. Having beaten Germany reserves (Austria) in their first ever European Championship game (1-0) the Faroes awaited an even bigger celebration. Then up pops Klose (which would have allowed some good *Sun* headlines if they could have been bothered) and Bobic in the 89th and 90th minutes. Germany 2-0 Faroe Islands; the score-line looks comfortable. It is a typically German 'effort' and why, even in these days of beating them 5-1 in

Munich,[24] all England fans await games against Germany with a mixture of expectation, hope and fear.

If Portugal is reaching the end of its golden generation, Germans will be looking to 2004 to signal the end of its 'not quite good enough' generation, just in time for the World Cup 2006 which they will controversially host ahead of South Africa and England (who held it last eight years before Germany last did in 1974). Although in the past we might look back on German teams and see an awesome array of powerful forwards, intelligent midfielders, imposing defenders and 'why did he punch that?' goalies, today it seems we merely see a team which is quite good. The fact that they were slightly peeved about Owen Hargreaves declaring himself English seems to confirm that.[25]

However, what characterises Germany down the years is not, necessarily, the great players and great teams. They have never captured the imagination in the way that Holland, Italy and Brazil have done (although the latter less often than the mythology would imply). No, what has characterised Germany is the ability to make the best of themselves. This is exemplified by Japan/Korea. We can moan all we want about the lucky Germans (oh don't worry, we will) and the fact that they didn't meet any kind of serious opposition until the final (promptly losing to them more heavily than England had when playing badly) but the fact is the Germans still made the final.

Before that tournament I ran some comments past a German friend; 2002 was about restructuring for the Ger-

24 1 September 2001 Finger-wagging Jancker 6, Owen 13, 48, 66, Gerrard 45, Heskey 74.

25 No actually Owen's quite good; this sentence included to cheer up the 43 Canadian soccer fans.

mans; they went to the World Cup without serious hopes and ambitions. He agreed. And yet they were not an outrageous amount of luck away from upsetting the Brazilians. A German team without high expectations and without an enormous amount of talent nonetheless reached the final.

Late equalisers and penalty shoot-out wins seem to typify the German spirit which, at least from the outside, manifests itself not as plucky determination under pressure but cold, aloof superiority. It is what Portugal don't have. It is what Spain don't have. It can be exemplified most easily by something which happened half a century ago, in the 1954 World Cup in Switzerland. Having lost 8-3 to the undisputed best team (Hungary) in an earlier round, the Germans still went on to beat them 3-2 in the final. Although in 1966 and 1976 the Germans lost finals of tournaments (England 4-2 after extra time and against the Czechs on penalties) on both occasions they had scored last-minute equalisers to take the game into the extra period.

One of the stories which might surprise one most about the Germans was alluded to in the introduction. A Guardian survey, confirmed by Herr Karsten Hubscher's personal interview with Dieter Eilst, compared the alcohol consumption allowed by players of the various national teams in Euro 96. Many, I think England amongst them, were officially banned from alcohol consumption during the tournament, whilst others, one supposes, were allowed a glass of wine with meals. However, top of the boozing league, with two bottles of beer per day – preferably after training – were the *Deutscher Meister* who went on to win the tournament after depressingly coming from behind to beat the hosts, as they had done also on at least two other occasions.

Many of the German team play in Germany with a wider range of clubs represented than the relatively few teams which go to make up the England team, even if Sven has opted to choose the occasional player from Charlton or Southampton.[26] In recent times, international appearances have been made by players from Dortmund, Hamburg, Leverkusen, Bochum, Bayern Munich, Kaiserslautern, Schalke 04, Bremen, Hertha Berlin, Hanover, Wolfsburg, 1860 Munich and Stuttgart. Overseas teams – like England in recent times – have been few and far between in terms of providing players who represent Germany. Arsenal's impressive – though not always in a good way – juggler-in-chief Jens Lehmann and Liverpool's Dietmar Hamann are among the names likely to be most familiar. With two players from England having been represented in recent squads this makes England the overseas country to have contributed most players to the German team. This is hardly surprising when 13 German teams have been represented with Bayern Munich, Werder Bremen, Bayer Leverkusen and Borussia Dortmund contributing several players each.

Prediction

So, even in decline, Germany managed to reach the World Cup final in 2002, and though hardly impressive – or stretched – in qualifying, I guess we really cannot anticipate that they will roll over for anyone this time, more than any other time. If they get the right draw and a bit of

---

26 Actually this turns out not to be true, such is the extent to which Sven has handed out new caps in friendlies and to players outside the big clubs. See England section.

luck they might make the semi-finals...at which point you wonder if they might make the final...and so on. All of that said, I can't see Germany actually lifting the trophy this time around.[27]

Inevitable quarter finalists or surprise semi-finalists.

 ## **Germany** Quick Quiz

1 *'What is green and smells of fish?' – although in German obviously – is a German football song. True or false?*

2 *'Take those little leather shorts off.' – although in German obviously – is also a German football song. True or false?*

3 *Germany struggled with two last-minute goals to win their away qualifier against the Faroes (124th in the world). Did they also struggle in the home leg?*

4 *Why can we say that Germany had a 'close' shave in both games versus the Faroes?*

5 *So what happens when they come up against decent opposition then?*

6 *How many German players are called Fritz or have 'von' in their name?*

Nice shirts, shame about the hair

Italy

How pleased were you by Italy's controversy-riddled exit from the World Cup? Marvellous, eh? I say this partly to annoy one particular Man U supporter I know, who I refer to as Man U to annoy several other Man U fans I

27 In fact, should a situation arise where they reach the final I would probably only watch Germany play if it was against England. And if they were to win that game I don't think the TV would remain on for the presentations. So not only can't I see the Germans winning, I absolutely refuse to!

know. But I also mention it because don't the Italians just take themselves *far* too seriously?[28] It's the old 'you used to be a big club' syndrome, made famous by Nottingham Forest fans, but applied to the international scene. These days they are 'quite good' I'll grant you, but despite a tolerable tournament record they're nowt but a team of hatchet style butchers and diving prima donnas who at various points have been outshone by either England, Germany or France at international level and who currently wouldn't even be favourites against Spain, Portugal or England – and maybe not even Wales against whom they got their qualifying campaign off to such an inauspicious start.

OK, OK that may be a little harsh, but there is a little of the 'God given right' about Italy, whose fans are prone to the same delusions as England fans in believing their team to be the very best in the world – whatever mere statistics say! True, they almost did, and should have, won Euro 2000 and if I'm honest (which is a rare characteristic of anyone writing about football) then they probably do have a better record than England. But if ever another country was going to sing about 'oh so nears' it is this one. They lost on penalties in World Cup 1994 after a 0-0 bore draw versus Brazil; Roberto Baggio's spot kick miss allowing the altogether more modest talents of Dunga to lift the cup. And, in 1990, on a seemingly unstoppable course to the final as host nation, they stumbled over Argentina despite taking the lead. However, when they do get it right – as they did superbly in 1982 – they really are unstoppable. Perhaps a return to the Iberian peninsula, scene of

28 Exemplified by Perugia's threat to sack their Korean player for being rubbish all season and then knocking them out of the World Cup!

that earlier triumph, will inspire them this time.

Like Germany, Italy has a squad made up of players from a wide variety of local Serie A teams. All the following teams have provided players for the national team in the recent past: Juventus, Roma, Internazionale, AC Milan, Lazio, Atalanta, Chievo Verona, Bologna, Empoli, Parma and Perugia. This list of 11 isn't quite as extensive as the 13 home-based clubs who have provided players for Germany but it ain't bad. In fact scanning down the list for players earning a living abroad who has turned out for Italy recently and we find just the rather hopeless Massimo Maccarone of Middlesbrough, who has so far picked up just two caps. Given three other Massimos in the squad perhaps this was a case of mistaken identity.

At the time of writing, Italy's form in 2003 has been impressive in both friendlies and European qualifiers. Although they did drop points home and away to Serbia and Montenegro, this form was more than enough to see them comfortably home as group winners after they had initially struggled, with defeat in Cardiff and a home draw against Serbia and Montenegro (at the time playing as Yugoslavia, I believe).

Prediction

Italy are often uninspiring in a tournament's early stages. In 1982 they failed to win any group matches at all but went on to lift the cup. In 1996, although winning their first game, they were then eliminated, many believe through complacency. And so, much will depend on whether the Italians negotiate their group. If they do – and depending on how the draw works out – they are potential finalists as much as England, whether or not

they are playing well at the start of the tournament.
Semi-final at least.

 Italy Quick Quiz

1   *Italy's recent home friendlies – for instance v Slovenia, Turkey, Portugal and Northern Ireland – averaged more or less than 20,000 attendance?*

2   *At the time of writing (19.24 on 5 November 2003) who was the last player to score for Italy whose name does not end in a vowel?*

3   *Who on earth is Akhmedov?*

4   *Oh that's just cheating isn't it?*

5   *OK then, are there any players in the Italian team whose name does NOT end in a vowel?*

6   *Who scored most goals and in most matches for Italy during qualifying?*

Was 2002 just a blip?

France

Despite Japan/Korea 2002 France will go into these European Championships buoyed up by an absolutely outstanding run of results and as favourites. After trailing 1-0 for 25 minutes in Cyprus in the first qualifying match and barely escaping with a 2-1 win many were suggesting that France's day was done. However, they won the remaining qualifiers – all seven – scoring 27 more goals and conceding just one. They also bagged the Confederations Cup and –since Tunisia just after the last World Cup – has anyone really looked like beating them?[29] So what of their chances this time and what of my right to judge?

Well, I was somewhat non-committal before the tournament (in Japan/Korea) but did predict Senegal to produce the biggest shock and they didn't let me down.

Perhaps a sign of French strength – although more likely a sign that their domestic game is not very good – is that whereas most German players play in Germany, the Italians in Italy and the English in England, the French are spread out though Europe's best leagues: England is perhaps the most popular destination (you complain about the food but you're happy to take the money then?) with 12 recent French players playing mostly for Manchester United or Arsenal, but others too. England is followed by Spain (three), Italy (five) and Germany (two). Fourteen players who have played in recent games play in France but many of these only occasionally or as substitute.

The novelty of success hasn't worn off for the French with international friendlies attracting crowds in excess of 50,000 on a regular basis, and as a nation which produces an irritating range of sporting success at other sports such as rugby and tennis, they will be hopeful again in Portugal. On paper, at least, nothing should stop a team who could field Barthez, Silvestre, Gallas, Desailly, Petit, Viera, Makelele, Wiltord, Cheyrou, Pires and Henry just from its English-based players. But let's face it, this is a country without footballing tradition, history or passion; as ever it would be a shame for them to win. And as my wife – looking over my shoulder as I write – points out, what this book really needs is more stuff about how super England are. So that's your lot on France.

29 Erm..yes, actually: they lost 2-0 at home to the Czech Republic on 12 February 2003 but so
unlikely a result was this that in research I actually recorded the score the wrong way round. A bit
like that time when the papers assumed England had beaten the USA 10-1, although different.

Prediction

On the grounds that I am hopeless at predictions, I predict France to get to the final, although alas I mean it. No other team seems capable of putting together such fluent football. At best they seem a wonderfully oiled machine. However, on the flip side, when the oil runs low they do seem to misfire badly allowing hope for other teams. They fired at the right time in France 1998, despite near elimination by Paraguay, and they fired at the right time (and with no little luck) in Euro 2000. This time expect class to carry them to the final and luck to finally run out (hopefully against England).

    Finalists.

 France Quick Quiz

1 *In the twelve months from 12 October 2002 to 11 October 2003 in what percentage of their games did France find the net three times?*

2 *In what percentage did they not concede a goal?*

3 *Despite conceding only two goals in qualifying, France in fact trailed in two games in European qualification. One was in the 2-1 win in Cyprus. When was the other occasion?*

4 *In what percentage of European qualifiers did Thierry Henry find the net and how many times was that in total?*

5 *Was Thierry Henry France's top scorer in European qualification then?*

6 *Who takes France's penalties?*

Neither, I want it for my armpits

Sweden

Ah, the arrogant Swedes...or at least to their neighbours the traditional regional super power is regarded thus, although unlike the English, Sweden was rather quicker at giving other people their countries back rather than inventing the United Kingdom of Scandinavia and Southern Finland...*[Editor's note: Is this actually relevant? No? Well get on with it then!]* OK, OK, I was only setting the context as Sweden being a bit like Nottingham Forest – you know, you used to be a big club. You'd think I'd know better than to write this living in Nottingham and all, but as far as I'm concerned, there's only one team in Nottingham and that's County. Actually if 'You Pies' have folded by the time you read this, there might only be one team in Nottingham...let's hope not eh... that would be a disaster. *[Editor's note: I'm warning you, this is supposed to be about bloody Sweden!]*

OK, it is thought that the area currently known as Sweden was settled by nomadic herdsmen from Europe escaping hordes moving in from the Russian Steppes as early as 3000 BC...*[Editor's note: Do you actually know anything whatsoever about Swedish football ?]* Of course, only kidding... They are one of many sporting nations to begin with the letter S – Slovenia, South Africa and Senegal to name but a few – and got to the World Cup final in 1958 and reached the semi-finals and came third in 1994. They last lost to England in 965. *[Editor's note: He might mean 1965 rather than 965 but it's difficult to be sure; it was a long time ago!]*

Two things confuse people most about Sweden, apart

from their rich history and political structures which apparently this editor is not interested in. One is, why have they got it in for Poland? In qualifying for Euro 2000 they beat Poland twice, including the game which saw England sneak into the play-offs because of their superior record versus the Poles. Then in qualifying for Portugal they beat Poland twice and then lost at home to Latvia when victory would have seen the Poles themselves qualify for the play-offs by virtue of their head-to-head record v Latvia! The second thing is why Anders Svensson looks so bloody good for Sweden but never really seems to fulfil his potential in a Saints shirt. Irritating, that.

A large number of players have represented Sweden in recent times, which suggests more about experimentation than a surfeit of talent. Many of these players play abroad, but also many for clubs which sound unfamiliar even after years of following European football: Djurgardens? Orgryte? Landskrona? Sundsvall? Everton?! Many others play for the established Swedish giants like Malmo, AIK Stockholm or Halmstads or in neighbouring Denmark and Norway. Dotted around Europe you will also find the odd Swede – and in Freddy Ljungberg's case a very odd Swede – in Scotland, England, Portugal, Germany, France and Holland. By far the best of these is Michael 'Killer' Svensson of Southampton, although again how one can be so accurate with defensive headers and then miss the chances he has, is baffling! *[Editor's note: Apart from Southampton having a couple of Swedes, I'm still not convinced he knows very much about Sweden at all. So for all the information you need, please consult www.svenskfotboll.se, where you'll find all the latest news, facts and figures – in Swedish, I'll grant you...]*

Predictions

By now we have come to expect Sweden to have a good team but not a very good team. Even when they exceed expectations, however, we never really think they will be quite good enough. So it will be again this time, although they do have the talent to reach the quarter-finals and once there anything can happen. If you want to pin me down – and I think the editor's beginning to twig that I'm making this up – then I'd go for group stage elimination.

Eliminated at group stage. Quarter-finalists on a good day. Semi-finalists on a very, very good day. Finalists on an exceedingly good day. Winners on the kind of day when you stuff the millions you just won betting on seven at the casino in your pocket, climb into your sleek hundred and seventy grand Ferrari, drive back to your penthouse suite with your super-model girlfriend, pop the most expensive champagne in the world and then – just as she's slipped into her sexiest underwear – seven of her mates arrive asking if they can join in...so an unbelievably good day in other words.

 Sweden Quick Quiz

1   *True or false? Sweden was settled by nomadic herdsmen from Europe escaping hordes moving in from the Russian Steppes as early as 3000 BC.*

2   *True or false? If the publishers wanted a serious football book they should have stumped up some more cash and got Brian Glanville or someone to write the book?*

3   *But do you think they'd have got anyone else to do it for the same cash in vitually no time at all?*

4　Is Skoog the name of a rather ornate lamp available at Ikea or the player who scored Sweden's goal on 18 February 2003 in a 1-1 draw with North Korea?

5　The game referred to in the question above was in something called the King's Cup. On 22 February the same teams contested the final. What was the score and how many did old Skoogy-doo bag himself this time?

6　Who top-scored for Sweden in qualifying?

Representing all that is good and decent in the world

England

How can you lie there and think of England when you don't even know who's in the team?

Billy Bragg

Something that every football fan knows: it only takes five fingers to form a fist.

Billy Bragg

You could intellectualise these quotes if you will, as some kind of comment on the dominance of hegemonic masculinity amongst England fans – and good luck to you if you know what that means any more than I do – but I put them there mainly because it's the sort of thing we authors do, and also because you really should go and dig out those old Billy Bragg records, or even update your collection with a CD purchase. They're surprisingly catchy and you can sing at least as well as he can.

Returning to football and the section title, despite a history of colonialism which has often caused the English to take this self-view – although one ought to add that the Scots were dis-proportionally represented in the British Empire – it is not one which is widely held. And whilst our current role as arch-apologists for the United States evil global project *[Editor's note: You should be thankful we restricted him to that! We had to delete all sorts of 'US is a terrorist state', 'human rights abusing hypocrite' stuff!]* may make us even less popular, it is really the reputation of our football supporters which Saatchi and Saatchi would have most trouble putting a positive PR gloss on. Even so, it does seem like a self-fulfilling prophecy in which England attracts dick-heads. I find those 'diary of a hooligan' books a bit tedious, but there's plenty of them out there if you want to research this assertion.

In short, England has a very good team, an excellent 'fighting' record[30] in competitive football and it really would be a crying shame if all that was jeopardised this time, more than any other time, and so we'd better hope the authorities find a way, find a way to stop the fighting etc. Travel in Europe does not inspire one with confidence (we Saints fans are experts after a trip to Romania!). Intelligent policing seems to be replaced by the 'maximum number of riot police theory' tried and tested (to destruction) in Italy and Argentina for instance.

Anyway, England does have an exceptional array of talent, well managed, although how any of that explains Francis Jeffers and Paul Konchesky having an England cap I don't know. Jamie Carragher has more England caps than Matt Le Tiss!? I guess if friendlies in his day had been used to involve changing the entire team every

---

30 By 'fighting record' I don't mean that they actually start fights, but that they are good at coming from behind. Oh, and by 'good at coming from behind' I don't mean...
[Editor's note: Censored]

15 minutes we might have seen the God-like one in an England shirt more often but even so, that must strike you as odd. Anyway, with talent available down the middle with Campbell at centre-half, with Beckham in midfield and Owen up front, if other players can come through we must have a real chance.

As with the past, most England players play in England. The fate of Steve MacManaman may have dissuaded others from going abroad, although if David Beckham impresses the Spaniards with his work rate and skill as he appears to be doing, others may feel inclined to follow suit. Sven has changed a lot the days when England teams picked Arsenal's defence, Manchester United's midfield and Liverpool's attack plus Emile Heskey. In fact, when I began writing this, and in view of the old Man U, Arsenal, Liverpool (with a Leeds sub) selection process, I thought Germany's record of having 13 Bundesliga teams represented at international level in recent times was quite exceptional. I was also impressed with Italy's 11 although I did know that many more English teams now provide players for the national squad. In fact, in recent times players from Manchester United, Liverpool and Arsenal, obviously, but also West Ham, Leeds, Middlesbrough, Southampton, Blackburn, Chelsea, Newcastle, Aston Villa, Tottenham, Charlton, Birmingham and Everton have all represented England! That's 14 Premiership teams and one West Ham.

At the World Cup England showed promise, especially when you consider that before Sven took over we had lost at home to Germany and drawn away to Finland, making even qualification look a long way off. England had then won in Germany 5-1 (have I mentioned this before?) and showed that fighting spirit in securing the point needed against Greece. Again in qualifying England were impressive (see previous chapter) recovering from deficits in many qualifying games and holding on to 0-0 in Turkey despite having no fans.

Prediction

England will be – without a shadow of a doubt – one of the best teams at the tournament, with only France being of the calibre you would expect to defeat England more often than not. Accordingly, given the manager we were denied in 1992 and 2000 and the luck denied in 1996 we should really go all the way.

Finalists. Possibly winners. Although much will depend on Campbell, Beckham and Owen, we also need Calamity James to continue error free, Bridge to oust the liability Ashley Cole, Lampard to continue his impressive (even unlikely) improvement and Rooney (possibly even Joe Cole) to develop through to the championships.

 England Quick Quiz

1   Who is the greatest number 7 recently to represent England?

2   Which game drew the biggest crowd and smallest crowd of the following European Championship qualifiers? England 2-0 Turkey, England 2-0 Liechtenstein, Turkey 0-0 England?

3   Who scored more goals in European qualifying for Portugal 2004, David Beckham or Michael Owen?

4   Who scored the penalties and how many were there?

5   Apart from Brazil in the World Cup England have lost few games in recent times. However one such defeat was 3-1 to

Australia. Despite fielding Jeffers and Konchesky amongst
11 half-time substitutes do the Aussies nonetheless believe
they are better than us?
6   *Where you come from, do they put the kettle on?*

Back from the brink

Bulgaria

Seems like an eternity ago. You remember don't you,
1994...that baldy bloke and Bulgaria beating the Germans? Well after that, Euro 1996 turned out to be a bit of
a disappointment and Bulgaria were in danger of slipping
off the footballing map and becoming more famous for
cut-price resorts on the Black Sea which you really should
get to before they're spoiled – so they say. But now, here
they are...finishing ahead of Belgium and Croatia in
Group 8, with both those teams ranked in the world top
20 while Bulgaria languish – barely inside the top 40 at 39.

And all this seems to be down to none other than Plamen Markov. Who? Precisely! And that's what they were
saying in Bulgaria itself about a man whose successful
(though not outstanding) international playing career was
mostly followed by managing Bulgarian second division
teams with household names like Chardafon Gabrovo, FC
Minion and Vidima-Rakovski – household names, always
supposing you have a house in any of those places.

But despite initial measured criticism which one might
loosely translate as 'what the f***ing hell did we choose
this Markov loser for?', 'Pla' as he is possibly known to
his friends has organised the best of the old with up and
coming youngsters into something resembling a football
team. Players such as Dimitar Berbatov of Bayer Lev-

erkusen and Georgi Peev of Dinamo Kiev give them half a chance combined with up and coming youngsters from Levski and CSKA of Sofia. Predicted to be the big disappointment of Euro 2004, however, will be Svetoslav Todorov – any player good enough for Pompey isn't good enough for me.

Rumour has it that Markov is a little disappointed about the international retirement of Krassimir Balakov at age 37. As to the footballing merits of the individual I really couldn't care less, but along with Seaman it is another potential comedy commentary moment gone from the game. Let's just hope that Paraguay's Chiqui Arce is still playing in Germany 2006 and that Swiss success continues so we have more of Bernt Haas.

Prediction

Having disappointed in Euro 96 and not arrived at Euro 2000 Bulgaria will be keen to do better this time around. However the missing sweet left-foot of Balakov and the early retirement (age 28) of Charlton's Radostin Kishishev in order to concentrate on his club commitments may leave the Bulgarians a little short, especially in defence. Though they have plenty of attacking options it is doubtful they have the necessary guile to break down the toughest defences whilst at the same time having potential vulnerabilities at the back.

Eliminated at the group stage.

 Bulgaria Quick Quiz

1 *How many goals did Dimitar Bebatov score in qualifying from Group 8?*

2   *Why did Belgium care more about Bulgaria's one defeat in
    Group 8 than Bulgaria?*
3   *How many Bulgarian players of recent times have names
    which do not end in the letter 'v'?*
4   *True or false? In recent times, Bulgarian home friendlies
    have attracted crowds below 10,000 whilst their European
    Championship qualifiers have averaged over 40,000.*
5   *Oh, it's really bugging me, what was the name of that
    bald bloke from 1994?*
6   *Great Uncle Bulgaria is the mascot of AFC Wimbledon (i.e.
    the real Wimbledon with real supporters). False or false?*

Bloody hell, how did they get here?

Greece

Who can forget Greece's performance in the World Cup
in 1994? Well me, for one, and I suspect most of Greece
too. I seem to remember the US Greeks getting very
'whoopy' – as Americans tend to – and excited, but that's
about it. They played Nigeria, perhaps somebody East
European and lost two games 4-0 and ended up with a
playing record of played 3, lost 3, for 0, against 10. And
now, 10 years later on they are ranked 26 in the world?
That's 13 above Bulgaria! And them, and their bald bloke,
I do remember from 10 years ago. Have Greece ever qualified for a major tournament since? I don't think so, and if
they did it was even less memorable than 1994.

At this point I should say that some of my friends are
Greek and I know that when they're not ordering
women around they are a fiercely proud people. Because
of that I don't want my message to be misunderstood. I

have nothing against Greeks (very nice of the George Clooney look-a-like to watch Beckham's free-kick fly in) and find their country and its cheese pies (but not Retsina – ugh!) delightful. But let's get one thing absolutely clear - your football team is absolutely and completely bloody rubbish.

Greece's qualification was, indeed is, remarkable. Much of the story is outlined elsewhere in this book. But rather than look at that story again, let us instead look at goals scored by group winners as a league table.

```
France . . . . . . . . . . . . . . . . . . . . . . . . . . . . . . 29
Czech Republic . . . . . . . . . . . . . . . . . . . . . . 23
Sweden . . . . . . . . . . . . . . . . . . . . . . . . . . . . . 19
Italy . . . . . . . . . . . . . . . . . . . . . . . . . . . . . . . 17
Denmark . . . . . . . . . . . . . . . . . . . . . . . . . . . 15
Switzerland . . . . . . . . . . . . . . . . . . . . . . . . . 15
England . . . . . . . . . . . . . . . . . . . . . . . . . . . . 14
Bulgaria . . . . . . . . . . . . . . . . . . . . . . . . . . . . 13
Germany . . . . . . . . . . . . . . . . . . . . . . . . . . . 13
Greece . . . . . . . . . . . . . . . . . . . . . . . . . . . . . . 8
```

Eight! And of all those teams, only Denmark (9) and Switzerland (11) had a significantly worse defensive record. Only Switzerland's +4 goal difference was the same as Greece's. In Greece's defence (did they do anything else?), Norway only scored nine and Latvia 10 in reaching the play-offs and Bosnia-Herzegovina made seven goals go a long way but...

But...even Scotland got 12! This was a group with three teams ranked outside FIFA's world top 50. A group with Northern Ireland and Armenia, and Greece managed to win it with eight goals. Apart from the 2-0 thrashings of Armenia and Northern Ireland, Greece just kept beating people 1-0, after losing their first two games 2-0. And so, their record of six qualifying wins and 18 points, is bettered only by France (eight wins, 24 points), Czech Republic (seven wins, 22 points) and England (six wins, 20 points). So credit where credit's due but...

But...around 70% of qualifying teams (i.e. those in the tournament) scored more goals...including Cyprus, including Macedonia and including bloody Albania! Since I am about to explode with indignant disbelief, I suppose we should recognise that these were Euro qualifiers and Greece had a 'job to do'...and all credit to them, they did it averaging a goal a game. So what did their friendly results look like during that time?

Romania 0 – 1 Greece
Greece 0 – 0 Republic of Ireland
Cyprus 1 – 2 Greece
Greece 1 – 0 Norway
Austria 2 – 2 Greece
Greece 2 – 2 Slovakia

Hmmm...the Cyprus goal-fest is a bit misleading as the Greeks were 1-0 down to a penalty awarded by the (presumably Greek) Cypriot ref. But it is quite clear that Greece's tournament goal average is increased to a whopping 1.3 in friendlies, although playing the sparkling Irish and Norwegians is never going to help such averages.

So who are the players to produce such results. Household names? Well no, with the vast majority coming from Panathinaikos, Olympiakos and AEK in Athens

with the odd smattering from elsewhere, including Irak-
lis and PAOK Salonika, as well as Werder Bremen and
Hanover in Germany, Roma and Perugia in Italy and – of
course – Dimitrios Papadopoulos who, as well as winning
the stereotype name award – and at the time of writing
just one cap – plies (or plied) his trade at Burnley (which
is possibly the only mention they get in this book). Oh
and there's some guy called Dabizas newly arrived at
Leicester too and Stelios 'incredibly long other name
won't fit on his shirt' at Bolton.

Prediction

How can I put this without using the words 'crap'
'Greece' and 'are' in a different order? How about this
way...I look into my crystal ball. Ah yes the mists are
clearing. There's much optimism in Athens. Bars have
people crowding around television screens. Expectantly.
Oh, then I see a snowball. Yes it's definitely a snowball.
Oh, it's travelling away from me. Where's it going? Oh, I
can see a sign. It says 'Welcome to my home' and there's
a figure next to it. He has a tail and horns and is dressed
in red. The snowball passes him and into the house.
'Good luck,' I shout.

Eliminated at the group stage.

 Greece Quick Quiz

1 *True or false? Watching the Greek goalie who looks a lot
   like George Clooney on player-cam would be more entertaining than watching the real George Clooney in the film
   Solaris?*
2 *Do Greece's home crowds average over 10,000?*

3 *Beware of Greeks bearing gifts. True or false?*

4 *Who is Greece's top scorer from qualifying?*

5 *For whom does the Greek goal machine mentioned above currently turn out?*

6 *What is Stelios of Bolton's real name that won't fit on shirts, with a bonus point for the correct spelling?*

Every now and again, we make it

Switzerland

Ranked 43 in the world and only occasionally troubling the big boys of world soccer, it is perhaps surprising to see Switzerland having qualified for Portugal 2004. Part of the surprise for me is that they even bother to enter the tournament at all. After all, Britain and Denmark might be quite 'euro-sceptic' but neither can match the fanatical neutralism of Switzerland who aren't even properly in the United Nations such is their determination to remain aloof. Possibly they regard themselves as just too different to join in – certainly cuckoo clocks are weird – but actually this has precious little to do with football. *[Editor's Note: Again!]*

Part of the Swiss success might be that they have not experimented too much in recent times. No wholesale half-time substitutions here! Of course this might be a deliberate strategy to try and develop a settled side following recent disappointments, or else it might be that they just haven't got a great many talented players. Apart from Stephanie Henchoz, could you name me a current Swiss international player? I think there's your answer...? (Possibly those you might have named, if you did, would be the heavily capped Chapuisat (who!) and the European player most likely to rival Paraguay's Chiqui Arce for name that sounds most like some kind of bottom – West Brom's Bernt Haas).

Anyway, the point is that Switzerland were able to top a tricky– if not actually intimidating – looking group, managing to finish ahead of Russia (condemned to a trip to Wales), Eire, Albania and Georgia. The secret of their success came with their home form, where they achieved three of their four victories, including the crucial 2-0 victory over the Irish Republic. Away they managed only one win, against Eire – which also turned out to be crucial – drawing with both Albania and Georgia.

Prediction

Well, if they get a game against Greece then I wouldn't bet against them winning a game, and really they are capable of causing a surprise. However, I wouldn't recommend you back the Swiss, even though I have resisted the temptation to do lots of gags about their defence and cheese with holes in it.

Eliminated at group stage.

 Switzerland Quick Quiz

1 *Switzerland's only defeat in qualifying came away to Russia. What was the score?*
2 *What was the highest crowd Switzerland played in front of in getting to the finals?*
3 *Who was Switzerland's top scorer in qualifying?*
4 *Who is the most capped player in the Swiss team?*
5 *In which country other than Switzerland do many Swiss national team players earn a living?*

6 *Despite being land-locked, 'In the Navy' is still the most commonly played tune in Swiss discos to this day. True or false?*

Almost as difficult to write off as the Germans

Czech Republic

The Czechs won the European Championships in 1976, although in those days with the help of their friends and neighbours the Slovaks. In the final they beat the Germans on penalties. That is a fact I suspect I have mentioned elsewhere in the book and which I would be tempted to repeat several times, except the editors have got a bit wise to that 'joke' and threatened not to pay me if I keep wasting words by repeating all things anti-German. In any case, 20 years later when Germany had absorbed the former East Germany and the Czechs had agreed an amicable separation with the Slovaks, the Germans exacted revenge with a highly dubious 2-1 'golden goal' final victory.

Despite such facts, and a reasonable record in the World Cup (two finals, although in 1934 and 1962) the Czech Republic still seem to be regarded as dark horses in world soccer despite ranking 11 in the current FIFA standings. This time is probably no different with few people talking of them as serious contenders. In fact, so under-rated are they that when I was writing the French section of this book, there I was writing 'France fantastic blah, great record, blah blah' that I actually transposed the score for France v Czech Republic. The French were not unbeaten. They lost 2-0 at home to the Czechs in

February 2003. The Czechs also beat Serbia and Montenegro 5-0 in a friendly (the same team which held Italy and beat Wales twice each in qualifying) and Turkey 4-0.

The Czechs' qualifying record has been absolutely spectacular and second only to France. The only points dropped were away to Holland, where they recovered from a goal down to take a point. Additionally, and unlike France, they really haven't lost for a long time, trouncing opponents at will. Only the Dutch (1-1) and the Swedes in a 3-3 friendly draw have escaped undefeated. Given that they failed to qualify for the last World Cup – losing disappointingly in a play-off against Belgium – this form is all the more remarkable.

The odd thing is that whilst you might expect the 7-foot 8-inch tall Koller to knock in a few goals and Nedved to provide quality in midfield, you probably don't expect Vladimir Smicer (Vlad the Incapable), Milan Baros and Karel Poborsky to knock them in too. But that's what has happened as goals have come from all round the park; although admittedly most of Smicer's have come in friendlies, proving that he really is a small game player. In the qualifiers themselves, Koller scored six. Also on the score sheet were Nedved (2), Baros (3), Smicer (2), Jankulovski (3), Poborsky (2), Rosicky (1), Lokvenc (2), Stajner (1) and Vachousek (1). Ten outfield players getting on the score sheet in qualifying is very healthy indeed, and during the same period several others also managed goals in friendlies.

So, being able to score from anywhere and undefeated under their current coach (Karel Bruckner) the Czechs are in confident mood. The coach's appointment was interesting and controversial, Bruckner having been assistant to the previous incumbent Jozef Chovanec, who led the disastrous 2002 World Cup campaign and who had taken to personally criticising players. But although some players considered quitting the national team because of Bruckner's appointment (and Patrik Berger actually did; once again showing the exceptional judgement which took him to Fratton Park!) most stayed on and have been pleasantly surprised as morale has improved and as the new coach has successfully integrated players from the 2002 European Under-21 Championship winning team, including the inspirational performances of young Petr Cech in goal.

Prediction

When they make the finals, they usually don't muck about. The authority with which they beat Costa Rica 4-1 in 1990 for instance was most impressive, managing four times what the Scots failed to do at all. *[Editor's note: Absolutely gratuitous mention of that game again; we can only apologise and offer a full refund to anyone who can convince us that Scottish domestic football is exciting.]* But anyway, expect competence and perhaps the odd surprise; if Alexander Dubcek had hoped that Czechoslovakia could promote 'socialism with a human face' then the Czech football team very much represent the same grit, determination and efficiency that we have come to expect from the Germans, except that we quite like them.[31]

Quarter-finals but probably no farther.

---

31 All of this applies only unless they play England, in which case delete all the niceness.

Czech Republic Quick Quiz

1 *From August 2002 until the end of qualifying the Czechs averaged more than three goals per game. True or false?*
2 *What did they average in qualifying?*
3 *Such is the Czech-Slovak rivalry that a friendly match between the teams in August 2002 had a recorded attendance 11,985 above the official safety limit, leading to a European fine and closure of the Dubcek Stadium in Prague. True or False?*
4 *Roughly what percentage of current Czech capped players play their domestic football in the Republic?*
5 *Which Prague team provides the most players for the national team?*
6 *How many of the Czech goalkeepers and defenders at Euro 2004 are likely to have over 30 caps?*

Could you be more surprised?

Latvia

In the *World Soccer Yearbook* for 2003 all the other teams which went on to qualify are set out nicely, with photos, a whole page each (including record of appearances etc) and helpful formatting. The Latvians meanwhile are squeezed unceremoniously between Kazakhstan and Liechtenstein, with the information crowded together unhelpfully, safe in the knowledge that no one will ever want it.

A look at their results from recent times (excluding the impressiveness against Turkey) fails to excite. The season opened with a 0-0 draw against Azerbaijan (who seem incapable of performing at international level except against Serbia and Montenegro) and a 4-2 defeat to Belarus. Both those teams managed one win in qualification. Belarus scored as many in that game in Riga as they did in the whole qualifying tournament. Despite this, the qualifiers themselves began with a respectable 0-0 draw against table-topping Sweden. In fact Latvia are the only team to prevent Sweden scoring in qualifying, a feat they performed once again in Stockholm to ensure qualification. In fact, the four points Latvia took from Sweden, compared to the nil points that Poland managed turned out to be the crucial difference.

But after that first 0-0 draw no one would really have expected the Latvians to progress. Even after a 1-0 win in Poland, the same result in San Marino hardly gave the impression that they were likely to keep going, any more than you would have thought Wales would. And indeed the bubble did seem to burst. After then winning 3-0 at home to San Marino and taking the lead in Hungary, they then lost that game 3-1. When that loss was followed up by defeat at home to Poland (the 2-0 score-line meaning the Poles had aggregate advantage in any head-to-head points situation) it looked like the game was up.

However, a narrow home win against Hungary at least gave the Latvians a chance, but it still looked like they would need to get something in Sweden. And though they managed that, no-one then really expected them to beat Turkey, certainly not when trailing with 25 minutes to go in Istanbul! And all of this without the Latvian Michael Owen, Marian Pahars, who managed just a cameo role in qualification!

So who have they got then? Well you've possibly heard of Alex Kolinko? (Bench-warming goalie at Crystal

Palace). Or Igor Stepanovs? (former bench-warming defender at Arsenal). OK, Imants Bleidelis? (Erstwhile bench-warmer at Southampton, from whence he came at half time in the FA Cup tie v Tranmere which Saints led 3-0 at half-time and then lost 4-3). Well all of these players seem to have performed better for country than club, the only exception perhaps to this rule being Pahars when fit.[32] And one player you may now have heard of after the winner in Riga and equaliser in Istanbul is Maris Verpakovskis.

Prediction

Commentators everywhere, having practised those awkward Turkish names in 2002, are now cursing the qualification of Messrs Blagonadezdins, Zakresevskis, Kolesnicenko and Prohorenkovs et al. If Pahars is fit again, maybe just maybe, him and Verpakovskis can do the damage to take them even further. That would have to be an outside chance, but Latvia got a win and a draw against Turkey in two games and by my book that's impressive whether it's England or Latvia.

Eliminated at group stage, although likely to be everyone's second team.

 Latvia Quick Quiz

1   *With a goal roughly every four games, who is currently Latvia's top scorer in internationals?*
2   *Marian Pahars played for Skonto Riga before moving to Southampton. But can you name any other Latvian teams?*
3   *Latvia won three of their four away games in qualifying.*

32 At the time of writing Pahars is fit again and has the potential to out-pace almost anyone.

Which was their easiest and which the most difficult win?
4 *What does a Latvian flag look like?*
5 *In the play-off versus Turkey, Verpakovskis emerged as the goal-scoring hero, but in the qualifiers who scored the most out of Latvia's 10?*
6 *True or false? This is the first major footballing tournament that not only Latvia but any of the former Soviet Baltic republics have qualified for?*

Against slightly unfavourable odds

Croatia

After their first leg home draw against Slovenia, Croatia must have been ever such slight underdogs in the second leg despite their loftier world ranking. They became even more under-doggier after having Juventus' Igor Tudor sent off with half an hour remaining and still trailing on away goals. However, they won through to qualify for another major tournament in their relatively brief post-Yugoslav existence, which reached a peak in the 1998 World Cup quarter-final when they beat Germany 3-0, beat Germany 3-0, only to lose to 10-man France in the semis. However, and despite the win against Germany, they had largely lost popular support by that stage – France's 10 man-ness being due to some appalling and blatant play-acting by Slaven Bilic which led to Laurent Blanc missing the final.

It has to be said that the Croatia of today do not look capable of beating anyone 3-0. They look dour and dogged and if it wasn't for the recent emergence of the young Dado Prso scoring in both legs of the play-offs it is difficult to imagine they would have overcome Slovenia.

Fortunately, an away goal to the good, the Slovenians decided to be even more dour and had no answer once Prso had scored. In 30 minutes against 10 men they barely managed a shot, with seemingly no plan B in case of emergency.

Many of the Croatian team play for the relatively well known domestic teams of Hadjuk Split and Dinamo Zagreb as well as the slightly less well known Varteks Varazdin. The rest of the squad is spread all over Europe in Germany, Greece, Italy, Austria, Belgium, France and England as well as outside Europe in Israel in the case of Giovanni Rosso. Despite unhappiness with the coach and the team not being what it once was, Croatia still have a decent team. In recent friendlies they drew 2-2 with Macedonia (having trailed twice) and beat Sweden which makes them at least as good as England, wouldn't you say?

Prediction

Croatia no longer hold any surprises and – Prso notwithstanding – in the post Boksic and Suker days they appear to offer very little indeed. The shirts may still attract a certain novel charm but that's about all. Similarity of results with England notwithstanding, unlikely to progress. If they do it will probably be at the expense of England.

Eliminated at group stage.

Croatia Quick Quiz

1   *Dado Prso, play-off hero scoring both Croatia's goals, managed how many in qualifying?*
2   *Who scored most goals for Croatia in qualifying?*

3   *True or false? Dado Prso has the shortest name in the Croatian team?*

4   *Assuming Boksic not to be a part of the current Croatian squad, how many have got into double figures in terms of goals scored at international level?*

5   *Which current Croatian player has scored the most goals?*

6   *How many has the player in Question 5 scored and was this at a faster or slower rate than Latvia's Marian Pahars?*

Unlikely to impress in the finals

Spain

Apart from losing at home to Greece, Spain qualified relatively easily. True a 0-0 draw in Belfast forced them into a play-off, and true they trailed 1-0 at home in that and only just escaped with a win, but ultimately they cruised past a rather disappointing Norwegian side. However, and such was the case also in qualifying for Japan/Korea, cruising through qualifiers has never so much been Spain's problem as much as actually producing it on the big stage.

Spain are allegedly now ranked third in the world, but rather like recently inflated rankings for Colombia or the USA, no one will be particularly quaking. Unlike those other teams of course, Spain really do have enough talent that other teams ought to be quaking. In a pattern the reverse of France, all of these talented players are currently playing in Spain with club representation in the Spanish squad, at the time of writing roughly as follows:

Real Madrid (7)
Deportivo La Coruna (5)
Valencia (5)
Barcelona (4)
Betis (3)
Real Sociedad (3)
Athletic Bilbao (2)
Atletico Madrid (2)
·Celta Vigo (1)
Valladolid (1)
Malaga (1)
Espanyol (1)

Raul Bravo's temporary spell at Leeds in 2002/03 is the exception which proves this rule. The big question is whether all the great players we are talking about can produce the goods in Portugal. The answer, as always, is almost certainly 'no' as we watch talented individuals freeze on the big stage. Is it the political structure of Spain such that the different nationalities (Basque, Catalan etc) do not feel really Spanish and therefore lack sufficient passion? Actually who cares as long as they don't suddenly sort it out if they should face England!

Prediction

Unlikely to have the support of many Portuguese neutrals, but should get through the group stage. Despite their world ranking, Spain hardly look like world beaters when it matters and time and time again they have proved they are not!

Will get through group stage. Won't get to final.

🏃 **Spain** Quick Quiz

1 *Despite Wales' impressive average crowd during qualification, Spain played in front of the largest crowd in qualification. Against which team?*

2 *How many goals did Raul score in the qualifiers at group stage?*

3 *Ruben Baraja scored twice against Northern Ireland. What other important goal did he score in qualification?*

4 *Spain scored 16 goals in qualifying. How many were scored in the first half?*

5 *Of the four goals Spain conceded in qualifying how many were in the first half?*

6 *How did Spain lose at home to Greece in qualifying?*

It'll only cause more arguments

The Team Spirit of Holland

Being edged out by the Czechs and then losing in Glasgow probably pushed the Dutch closer to elimination than they would have hoped. This probably caused more arguments, possibly when someone on the bench in Glasgow started sniggering when the crowd started singing 'he's bald, he's fat, he's gonna get the sack, Advocaat.' The Dutch are great at arguments. Given the talent they have – Holland B would have beaten Scotland in a play-off – one wonders what they might achieve if they stopped trying to be more arrogant than the Germans[33] and started pulling together. After missing out on Japan/Korea, failure to beat the Scots and qualify this time would probably

---

33 As football genius Berti Vogts pointed out, German 'arrogance' is German 'confidence' and in their case is usually directed towards a team effort.

have meant a third world war in the Dutch camp.

No one has ever really worked it out but the Dutch just don't seem to be able to play nicely together. Thus the list of talent is amazing from back to front: Van der Sar, De Boer, Cocu, Zenden, Overmars...all hugely talented, with the possible exception of Boudewijn. And the strikers! OK, so most of them have personality 'issues' but what a selection! Patrick Kluivert has been the most successful at international level, but then they've got some bloke called Van Nistelrooy, plus Roy Makaay, Jimmy Floyd Hasselbaink and Pierre Van Hooijdonkey! Wow! The trouble is Patrick doesn't like Ruud and Jimmy doesn't like anyone – that kind of thing. Rumour has it that Pierre stole Roy's comb and Pierre will only play with Patrick if it's a midweek fixture. Hey, who knows what's going on?

Unlucky to have to go through the play-offs thanks to coming up against the resurgent Czechs, Holland then did well to win against Scotland despite Vogts' team putting up a spirited display in the first leg of the play-offs. In friendlies over the past year Holland have drawn with 2004 hosts Portugal and thrashed Germany 3-1 away with Kluivert, Hasselbaink and Van Nistelrooy all getting on the score sheet. The Dutch actually seem to get more pleasure out of beating the Germans than we do. If they can just get along like good children now...in several tournaments since 1970 Holland have had the best team and not won. In terms of talent, once again this time they are potentially as strong as France and Spain.

As you would expect of such a relatively small country with such talented footballers, the Dutch squad play their club football all over Europe in the following countries: England, Spain, Scotland, Germany and Italy as well as Holland itself. Surprisingly there are no Dutch internationals in France or Belgium.

Prediction

Having got there Holland are unlikely to be a big flop, but similarly unlikely to really go all the way. That said, the European Championships are possibly more their thing than World Cups. Expect this vast array of talent to reach the quarter-finals even if the manager is sulking and none of the players are talking to each other by then. Don't be surprised if they reach the semis even if certain players refuse to play on the same side of the pitch together. But don't bank on them getting any further. If they do, don't expect certain players to be prepared to celebrate with each other.

Get through group stage. Won't get to final.

 Holland Quick Quiz

1   *How many Dutch players have scored 10 or more goals for the national team?*

2   *The seven above does not include Jimmy Floyd Hasselbaink. True or false?*

3   *Which player, despite being prolific in domestic football, averages less than a goal per 10 games for Holland?*

4   *Who has the strangest first name in the Dutch team?*

5   *Why does Edgar Davids wear those funny things like glasses when playing?*

6   *While England were losing to Australia at football in February (who cares after the rugby!) who were Holland playing and beating?*

Russia

I may have added something subsequently, but it may be significant that I couldn't really think of any headline to attach to Russia. Despite scoring a few at home, they qualified unspectacularly behind Switzerland thanks largely to an unexpected defeat in Georgia. In beating Wales 1-0 over two legs in a play-off they then showed themselves to be technically efficient but boring enough to bore even the staunchest football fan. But going back to even the 'great' Soviet sides efficiency has always won out over style.

In fact, the story of Russia's qualification is most odd. Two home victories with four goals each were followed by two away defeats to table proppers Albania (3-1) and Georgia (1-0). At this point Russia must have feared the worst, but fighting 'come from behind' draws away to Switzerland (2-0 to 2-2) and Ireland (1-1) put them back in with a chance. At that point they scored three and four in winning their final two home games, prior to the efficient elimination of Wales.

Famous names in the Russian team are few and far between, with the most famous players from that part of the world tending to be Ukrainian these days. Some will have heard of Beschastnykh even if they have trouble spelling it. Alexei Smertin may also have come to the attention of some readers following a misguided move to Portsmouth. Lokomotiv Moscow's endeavours in the Champions League have brought others to our attention, most notably Loskov.

Prediction

Tidy uninspiring football will only get you so far at international level, and in Russia's case it has probably already taken them as far as it will. They might possibly sneak through the group stage (though only as runners-up) but I wouldn't bet a great deal on such an outcome if I were you! Eliminated at group stage.

 Russia Quick Quiz

1 *Several of the Russian squad play for a team named after a planet. Which one?*

2 *Who does Denis Laktionov play for?*

3 *Which team provides most players for the Russian squad?*

4 *Which other teams from Moscow also contribute players to the national team?*

5 *Name some other teams in Russia who have international players.*

6 *What we need is a strong leader like Stalin to sort us out?*

7 *Russia?*

Where to go if this European Championship Guide has left you with a thirst for knowledge

If this hastily and randomly thrown together selection of facts leaves you yelling 'I must know more', here's where to go – although you may need to learn a foreign language first of course!

Bulgaria: www.bfunion.bg
Croatia: www.hns-cff.hr
Czech Republic: www.fotbal.cz
Denmark: www.dbu.dk
England: www.TheFA.com
France: www.fff.fr
Germany: www.dfb.de
Greece: www.epo.gr
Holland: www.knvb.nl
Italy: www.figc.it
Latvia: www.lff.lv
Portugal: www.fpf.pt
Russia: www.rfs.ru
Spain: www.rfef.es
Sweden: www.svenskfotboll.se
Switzerland: www.football.ch

Answers

Portugal

1: False. Portugal have qualified for three World Cups and three European Championships. The fact that they qualified for Euro 96 and Euro 2000, as well as the World Cup in 2002, means that in this context perhaps the 'golden generation' really have produced the goods after all!

2: Bolivia

3: True. On 2 April Herr Nobs refereed a 1-0 victory over Macedonia in a friendly played in Switzerland. Then on 30 April Herr Meier refereed a Portuguese friendly in Eindhoven against Holland

4: Actually I do not know Mr Ovrebo's first names but Odd and Bent are perfectly cromulent[24] names in Norwegian so it's entirely possible I guess

5: Outrageously true!

6: Fernando Couto and Luis Figo

Denmark

1: Eight

2: The fifth minute of injury time

3: Apparently not

4: Apparently so

5: Nobody, as they lost 2-0

6: Morten Olsen – he's famous in Denmark, OK?

Germany

1: True, a song of 'tribute' from Bayern fans to Werder Bremen

2: True, this being Bremen's frightening retort to the fish jibe above

3: Yes, it was 1-1 at half time and they scraped home 2-1

4: The winning goal in Germany and the go-ahead goal away were both scored by Miroslav Klose

5: Well apart from taking the opportunity to gratuitously mention the 5-1 match of 1 September 2001, in Germany's next two games after the Faroes home fixture they lost 3-1 to Holland (home) and then 3-1 to Spain (away) with Bobic grabbing a consolation on each occasion

6: None, so stop your stereotyping

Italy

1: Slightly less

2: Akhmedov

3: He scored an own-goal in Italy's favour while turning out for Azerbaijan

4: Yes it is

5: Yes, Buffon...but he plays in goal

6: Filippo Inzaghi scored six including a hat-trick against Wales but only found the net in three games. Del Piero's five goals were scored in four games

France

1: 60%

2: 80%

3: They went 1-0 down to Israel away, on that occasion also coming back to win 2-1

4: 50%, six goals

5: Yes and No. Sylvain Wiltord also bagged six

6: Against Malta Zidane, against Colombia Henry and against Japan Pires – apparently

Sweden

1: Unless it was a very lucky guess, false

2: True

3: Precisely my point

4: I would hope you'd heard of Niklas Skoog of Malmo

5: Sweden 4-0 North Korea including goals by Skoog in the third and 77th minutes

6: Marcus Allback with five

England

1: David Beckham, but only because they gave the number 10 shirt to Matt Le Tiss

2: More than 64,000 saw England struggle past Liechtenstein at old Trafford. More then the 48,000 at the stadium of Light for Turkey and the 42,000 packed into Fenerbahce stadium in Istanbul

3: They both scored five

4: Beckham got two penalties and Owen one. And of course there was the one that was spectacularly missed...

5: Yes, but the Ashes will be ours, oh yes, they will

6: La la la, and we all like vindaloo, we're gonna score one more than you, England!

Bulgaria

1: Five

2: It came in Bulgaria's last game; Bulgaria had already qualified and it allowed Croatia to make the play-off's instead of Belgium on the basis of the record between the two teams

3: Just the three, Pazin, Zagorcic and Jankovic

4: True. 21 August 2002 and 10,000 watch a friendly draw against Germany whilst two games later 42,000 watch tiny Andorra pour forwards for an equaliser as Bulgaria hold on to a 2-1 victory and

---

24 Cromulent is not a word; you'll need to watch The Simpsons too often to get this one!

three priceless points

5: *Please write to Dr Pettiford, c/o The Department of International Studies at the Nottingham Trent University and put him out
of his misery! – Ed.* [32]

6: False

Greece

1: True. I mean have you ever seen that
complete drivel?

2: Just, but only because 15,500 glory
hunters turned out to see the spell-bind-
ing 1-0 qualification clinching game
against Northern Ireland. Was never
scoring goals part of the Good Friday
agreement?

3: Probably true. Gift-bearing Greeks must
be more dangerous than ones in front of
goal

4: Haristeas has tucked away three
including two in one game against
Northern Ireland

5: The best team in Germany, Werder
Bremen

6: Giannakopoulos

Switzerland

1: Russia won 4-1 although the Swiss took
the lead

2: 40,000 in their crucial win in Dublin

3: Frei got five

4: Stephane Chapuisat who – if he keeps
getting picked – will hope to pick up a
100th cap sometime around the time of
the finals

5: Germany with players at Hamburg, 1860
Munich, Werder Bremen, Freiburg and
Borussia Monchengladbach

6: False, it's YMCA

Czech Republic

1: True, 41 goals in 13 matches

2: Just under three at 23 goals in eight
matches

3: False, unless the Dubcek Stadium really
exists and has a capacity of one. In fact
11,986 turned up in total in Olomouc to
see the Czechs recover from a goal down
to win 4-1

4: About 50%

5: It's probably 50/50 between Slavia and
Sparta Prague

6: None. At the time of writing Marek
Jankulovski has the most caps from this
group with 22

Latvia

1: Marian Pahars with 15 goals in 56
matches

2: Thought not. Of the current squad at

least one comes from each of Metalurgs
Liepaja, Dinaburg Daugavpils and
Ventspils

3: Technically the 2-0 win in Poland was
most comfortable, while the 1-0 win in
San Marino came courtesy only of a last-
minute own goal

4: A white horizontal stripe on a red background

5: It was Verpakovskis again with four,
although Bleidelis scored three

6: True

Croatia

1: Just the one. Against Belgium

2: Nico Kovac and Milan Rapajic both
netted twice

3: True and false. Leko, Olic, Srna, Agic and
Bule all have only four letters in their
second name. Only Nino Bule however
can match the eight letter total and no
one is able to beat it

4: One

5: Goran Vlaovic

6: 15 in fewer games than a similar number
for the pacey Saints striker

Spain

1: Ukraine, 82,000

2: Five

3: The winner at home to Norway in the
play-offs

4: Just three

5: Two

6: Nobody really knows

Holland

1: seven

2: True, although he is on nine at the time
of writing

3: Roy Makaay

4: Edwin, Jaap, Wilfred, Edgar, Clarence,
Wesley or Arjen – probably

5: It's related to the condition glaucoma
but I'll not kid you I know all the details

6: Argentina through a Van Bronckhorst
goal in the last five minutes

Russia

1: Saturn

2: Suwon Bluewings in South Korea

3: CSKA Moscow

4: At least Spartak, Lokomotiv, Dinamo and
Torpedo

5: Zenit St Petersburg, Rotor Volgograd,
Kryliya Sovetov and Saturn of course

6: Vasily Yanaev, former defender of Stalin-
grad, now 92 and steadily sipping vodka
in small unwelcoming bar in a Moscow
suburb says 'yes'

7. I never even met her!

32 I remembered – Letchkov!

The Key Players

Many people would agree that Jimmy Greaves was the finest player of his generation. But when it came to England winning the World Cup of 1966 he was not the key player, Geoff Hurst was. Similarly, many people would agree that Matthew Le Tissier was the most talented player of his generation. Indeed what sane person could disagree? But when England cried out for a bit of creativity – or even a decent penalty taker – he was not there. A potentially key player, not even on the bench as part of the armoury. The point of this then is that the players selected below are not necessarily the team's best players (although many are included), but the players who will need to perform above their best, or to emerge this summer if their particular nation is really to go far in the tournament. (Anyone tempted to take the occasional Pompey related jibe too seriously should note that I personally stand shoulder to shoulder with Portsmouth fans, but only in the face of a common enemy – i.e. Australian cricket – as part of the Barmy Army).

Bulgaria

Dimitar Berbatov and the rest of the team

Currently playing for Bayer Leverkusen in Germany with around 25 caps and an impressive goals per game ratio of above one goal every two games, Dimitar Berbatov is quick and moves well and is perhaps the stand-out player of the Bulgarians. But for them to shine it will need several players to emerge as big time players in the same tournament. As for instances, Georgi Peev of Dynamo Kiev, the much improved Stilian Petrov and the attacking left-sided midfielder Martin Petrov (no relation of Stilian). As for the defence it looks vulnerable and the coach has had to experiment; he will need to be something of an alchemist if he is to get the blend right for 2004. But if he does, it will be very much a team effort in support of Berbatov.

Among possible 'late runs' into stardom might be Georgi Chilikov. Scoring 22 goals for Levski Sofia in 2002/03 he thus topped the scoring charts by five goals from his nearest rival in a 26-game season. He has now broken into the national team, scoring the first in Bulgaria's unimpressive 2-1 home win over Andorra for instance. At 26 he will be at or around his peak for the tournament if he can dislodge some of the more established forwards permanently. More of a gamble in terms of likely impact – in fact probably about 10,000-1 against to score the winner in the final in Portugal – is Todorov. No not the bloke at Portsmouth – goodness me, he must be about 1,000,000-1 against...no I mean Anatoli Todorov, an under-21 international who helped his club side Lovech to the Bulgarian cup final (where they lost to Chilikov's Levski).

Coach: Plamen Markov

 ## Very Quick Quiz

1   *The goal and performance of which Bulgarian saw Germany eliminated from USA 94?*

   a) Emil Kostadinov   b) Krassimir Balakov
   c) Stilian Petrov   d) Yucan Fukov   e) Letchkov

Croatia

The Unpronounceables

By which I mean Dado Prso and Dario Srna. The strength of the Croatian side is undoubtedly going to be maximised if the old guard of Boksic and Suker can be effectively replaced by the younger generation. At the moment the signs of this are somewhat faltering but not altogether discouraging as a tricky play-off tie against Slovenia was negotiated with all the style, grace and tension which might be displayed by a debutant high-wire performer.

Dario Srna hasn't long been in the national team and will be just 22 at the time of the tournament. He earned his call-up after banging in a hat-trick for the under 21s and went on to score the opener against Belgium (after nine minutes) in what turned out to be a decisive 4-0 qualifying victory, thus taking the Croats into the play-offs on head-to-head basis v Belgium, losing only 2-1 away. Not so much a goal-scorer, and more of a provider, Srna could be important in these championships and a worry for England.

Another young player who may yet emerge is Dinamo Zagreb's teenage star Niko Kranjcar, who captained his side to the Croatian championship at the age of 18 and despite being the youngest player in the division. We all know there are three paths ahead for the talented youngster. He will do one of the following: get his chance and take to it like a duck to water or get his chance and look hopelessly out of his depth or not get his chance thanks to overly conservative football management such that when he finally does it will be too late. That's what disgracefully happened to Matt Le Tiss, though not Owen and Rooney. In any case Niko has all the right attributes.

Oddly enough the real emerging talent for Croatia will be almost 30 by the time of the championships in Portugal. Dado Prso, also banging them in for Monaco – affording excellent limerick-writing opportunities as if that has anything to do with anything – was on the score-sheet (like Srna) in the crucial win against Belgium. Since then he scored both Croat goals in the 2-1 aggregate win against Slovenia in the play-offs. He is thus 'on the crest of a wave'; if he can ride it all the way to Portugal, he will need to score more crucial goals if Croatia are to do well.

Coach: Otto Baric

 Very Quick Quiz

---

*Change only one word and then rearrange the following into
a puerile limerick which doesn't quite scan:*

>There once was a man called Prso
>For the size of his banana
>Though he did get some stick
>Sticking out wherever he'd go
>Who played for his team Monaco

Czech Republic

Petr Cech

Recently promoted from the all-conquering Czech
under-21 team, Petr Cech must be the finest young goalkeeper in Europe, notwithstanding the shot-stopping
abilities of Iker Casillas of Real Madrid and Spain. At the
time of writing Petr is turning out for Rennes in France,
although he will surely attract interest from bigger clubs
in the future. His performances have instilled confidence
throughout the Czech team and he is the only keeper –
since the World Cup of course – to shut out the current
European Champions France.

You might be tempted to suggest that if players such as
Smicer and Poborsky can replicate the form they showed
in the Premiership it's not going to matter how poor 'old'
Petr plays! However, Smicer has always looked a different
proposition in a Czech shirt – or was that a check shirt.
Anyway, never mind Vlad the Ineffectual, it's the form of
Poborsky that might be of more interest. Despite the disappointment of his stay at Manchester United he is now
enjoying something of an Indian summer in the Czech

Republic. He returned to Sparta Prague from Italy as the league's highest paid player and has proved all the doubting Tomases (that's the Czech spelling not a typo) wrong. In his first season, Sparta regained the championship from arch-rivals Slavia by a single point.

Another 'golden oldie' is Pavel Nedved who had a fantastic season in 2002/03 for Juventus. Many feel that his team's Champions League final defeat to Milan was as a direct result of Nedved being suspended and Juventus missing his power, pace and finishing which he seems to have moved up, rather than down, a gear as he moves into his 30s. One really confusing thing about Pavel is why Barry Davies – unless he speaks Czech of course – seems to want to extract the same ridiculous noises out of 'Nedved' as he previous reserved for Ole Gunnar 'Solskjaer'? It's like some kind of demented 'Neee-ed-vee-ed' noise. Still, unlikely to put the man off.

Apart from Petr Cech, the Czech's have plenty of young talent. 2002's Czech young player of the year – one of the doubting Tomases – Hubschman is a solid defender. His successor as young player of the year Vaclav Sverkos is a forward with unfashionable Banik Ostrava for whom he scored 14 goals (second highest in the league) in 2002/03. Whether he is still with them by the time you read this may have much to do with his chances of breaking into the Czech national team – such is the way of the world alas. But one potentially to watch.

Coach: Karel Bruckner

🏃 Very Quick Quiz

Which is the correct pronounciation of Pavel Nedved's surname according to Barry Davies?
a) Noose Vacuum   b) Nobble Vash   c) Neeee-ed-veee-ed
d) Nedved   e) Melon

Denmark

Claus Jensen

Charlton favourite Claus may not be everyone's choice of key player, but in the absence of Stig Tofting's creative genius, not to mention the Laudrups, midfield is where Denmark will need excellent performances. Up front they have reliable strikers in Rommedahl, Tomasson and Sand but it is a player like Jensen – at the peak of his career in his mid twenties – whom they really need to have a special tournament. His record so far of five goals from a little over 20 caps is fine, but he may just provide that bit more and take the Danes further than people expect. You might say ditto Gravesen (Everton, looks 38 but will be 28), Jensen (Man City, 29) and Poulsen (Schalke 04, 24).

But perhaps it is also at the upper and lower range of Denmark's midfield that we need to look for inspiration? Someone you wouldn't really expect to be at the peak of their career by summer 2004 is Morten Wieghorst. In fact he will be 33. However, returning to Brondby from Celtic he has overcome injury as well as illness and won back his place in the Denmark team. It seems perhaps doubtful however that he will be a major force at these championships – although with Denmark you just never know. Also in the Brondby midfield and tipped to be the next Danish superstar is Thomas Kahlenberg. Given the freedom to roam by none other than Michael Laudrup (Brondby coach) Thomas (aged 21) has proved the doubting Niclases wrong. Having just been promoted to the Danish national team, the time is right for him to emerge in Portugal.

Coach: Morten Olsen

 ## Very Quick Quiz

Which of the following footballers looks most like Denmark and Everton's Thomas Gravesen?

  a) Uncle Fester   b) Paul Gascoigne   c) Peter Beardsley
        d) Thomas Gravesen   e) Lee Carsley

England

Wayne Rooney

Much has been expected from 'Roonaldo' and so far he has done pretty well. Living up to your potential week in week out is difficult for anybody in any job but for Wayne in the national spotlight it must be even more so. If he can keep playing well enough to justify selection, the tournament itself may well be the spring-board to super mega stardom. With a strong core to the team already existing in the shape of Campbell, Beckham and Owen, the 'unknown' quantity of Rooney may well be the added ingredient that makes all the difference.

Another less spectacular Wayne is Bridge. Hopefully his move to Chelsea, as well as being bloody irritating, will also improve his international chances. With an even temperament and solid defensive qualities, as well as an ability to get forward, he has the potential to set the nerves jangling less often than Ashley Cole. Another nerve jangler is David James. Since he appears to have emerged as Sven's choice ahead of Paul Robinson and others, we can only hope that 'Calamity' gets the errors out of his system and is either dropped before next summer, or continues to produce the form that allowed him two clean sheets against the Turks.

Coach: Sven Goran Eriksson

 ## Very Quick Quiz

When England win in Portugal, we will have achieved a unique feat of winning major championships in sports that matter in consecutive years. But can you remember what the score was when England won the Rugby World Cup of 2003 to do the first leg of this achievement?

a) Australia lost so who cares

b) England won so who cares

c) What makes the Aussies (whinging Matildas) really sore is that they actually played their best and got some really dodgy refereeing decisions and still lost

d) Australia 17-20 England

e) Australia 17-20 Engerland (after extra time)

France

Big Zidane and Little Zidane

Zinedine Zidane – a world-class player who played injured and consequently badly in the 2002 World Cup. At 32, Portugal 2004 may well be the last tournament at which he himself expects to be able to perform at or about his best. Many consider that France's failure in 2002 was mainly due to this man being unable to perform and he may well be the key to whether they turn things around this time. Zidane is the pivot around which all things attacking turn. Sylvain Wiltord looks a much better player for France than Arsenal and Thierry Henry and David Trezeguet (both averaging a little under a goal every two games but mainly because France score from everywhere!) thrive on the service Zidane provides.

With so many French players playing outside France and well known, it is to the French League itself – the imaginatively titled Ligue 1 – to which we must turn for potential surprise packages. Jerome Rothen of Monaco is one such player. He is a left-sided attacking midfielder who gets more than his fair share of assists. Now may just be the right time for getting into the French midfield. Despite the form of William Gallas, given the big sulk of Marcel Desailly, much the same might be said of the French back four with Lille's Eric Abidal pushing for a place too. In recent historical perspective, Lille having a player in the French team is akin to the likes of Birmingham, Charlton and Southampton having England internationals – only more so. Whatever, Abidal has impressed hugely in 2003/04 and has been favourably compared to Lilian Thuram, although rumours that he was to change his name to Erica so that they could both have girls' names were wildly exaggerated. It has been a remarkable turn-around for a player not long ago loaned to Lille from Monaco because no one wanted to buy him. Having declared his wish to leave Lille – ah such gratitude and loyalty – he may be playing for PSG (or a team near you) by the time you read this.

And, perhaps depressingly, France also have talent awaiting on the forward production line. Mourad Meghni – who will be 20 by the time of the tournament – is known as the 'Little Zidane' and not it must be said because he is balding in a more bizarre fashion than even Red Rum look-a-likey David Platt, but because he is incredibly skillful and has great vision. Eschewing France for Italy as a young boy he served an apprenticeship in the Bologna youth team before breaking into their first team and instantly being compared with former Bologna, Sampdoria and (did he really play for) Leicester (?) star Roberto Mancini – and not it must be said because he had a hairstyle that looked like it would have cost a woman £100 at a fancy salon. It is an outside shot – given a slight physique – but Meghni could emerge in this tournament and go on to be as famous as Ronaldo, although let's hope not for a silly tuft hairstyle and the best chipmunk impression this side of Santa Cruz de la Sierra.

Coach: Jacques Santini

 Very Quick Quiz

The French National Team includes players born in all of the following except which?

a) Algeria   b) Morocco   c) Kenya
d) Senegal   e) Toulouse

Germany

Rudi Völler

Having played in one of the most impressive German teams of all time, Rudi Völler has – with the exception of

Michael Ballack – inherited a pretty uninspiring bunch of players. However, it is a bunch of players he steered to the World Cup final of 2002. As he now tries to introduce a new generation of younger players such as Kevin Kuranyi of Stuttgart, much will depend on Völler's ability to make the right decisions in allowing Germany to make the best of what it currently has. So far Völler has been impressive, and resilient, after the 5-1 mauling by England. Germany are unlikely to under-perform, it's just a question of whether the basic talent is currently good enough. Most Germans think that 2004 is a question of having a team good enough to win again on home soil in 2006 and that 2004 is going to be won by France.

Ballack will still be the one genuinely world-class player they have. Whilst 'one man team' would be an exaggeration it must be said that Bayer Leverkusen fell apart without him and Bayern Munich absolutely strolled the championship of 2002/03 with him. Even playing in a relatively deep midfield role he got into double figures and continues to find the net for Germany including as penalty taker. Joining Ballack on the scoresheet for Germany's last Euro 2004 qualifier against Iceland was young Kevin Kuranyi of Stuttgart who took advantage of Sean Dundee's injury at domestic level well enough to earn his call-up to the German national team. He is one of the younger players that Völler wants to have embedded in the national set-up for 2004 and beyond.

Coach: The afore-mentioned Rudi Völler

🏃 Very Quick Quiz

---

1. Add the minutes to the names!
Owen   Gerrard   Owen   Owen   Heskey
(Answers: a) 13, b) 45, c) 48, d) 66, e) 74)
2. Spot the odd minute out? 6, 13, 45, 48, 66, 74

Greece

Panagiotis Kreonidis

Dubbed the Greek 'Wayne Rooney' this 16 year-old wonder kid – with a Greek father and American mother – has yet to feature in the Olympiakos first team. However, said to possess blistering pace, outstanding vision and a wonderful pair of feet he is the sort of player who dribbles round several players and lashes the ball into the roof of the net with glee. The only problem with Kreonidis, of course, is that he doesn't actually exist. I made him up. But if Greece are to have any chance whatsoever then they had better have a 'Wayne Rooney' up their sleeves somewhere. Sorry Demis Nikolaidis (current top scorer amongst the Greek national squad with 16 in 43 appearances) I just can't see you becoming the surprise name at Euro 2004, although Christos Patsatzoglou might become the unpronounceable name of the tournament.

(Such a pronouncement may seem harsh after the scare Greece gave England in qualifying for Japan/Korea, but that performance must be taken in context. A Greek team long since eliminated playing the best they have for ages against a nervy England. That game was the exception which proves the rule of Greek mediocrity. Of course, there are no easy games in international football – except Germany away – but whilst every team may spring a surprise performance [Paraguay almost knocked France out of the World Cup in 1998 way before the French beat Brazil so easily in the final!] Greece really haven't got the firepower and ability to be classed as a feared team.)

Greece's player of the year in 2002/03 was the player with the name which looks suspiciously like 'limber up a lot' (though what that's got to do with anything I don't know) Nikos Limberopoulos. With a goal every couple of games for Panathinaikos and about one every five games in his 40 caps he is a steady but unspectacular player. Similarly, Anestasios Agritis hasn't had a bad season and at 23 shows a bit of promise. But really, this is an international tournament; not bad, steady and promising will not be enough. Oh Panagiotis Kreonidis where for art thou, and when we find you will anyone who knows how to pronounce your name properly?

Coach: Otto Rehhagel

 ## Very Quick Quiz

Greeks are better at all of the following than they are at football except? (This is a serious-ish question)

a) Weight-lifting b) Basketball c) Great food
d) Ancient civilizations e) Rugby

Holland

Don't be Ruud, Dick

How they manage to do it is beyond me, but the Dutch

just keep churning out players capable of fantastic skill, great goals and accomplished defending. At times the football they play is amazing; as near as Europe is going to get to Brazil and a far, far cry from the neighbouring dour Germans in the park with leather shorts for goalposts etc. They also seem to have a self-destruct switch which allows them to create arguments at will over topics as important as who's got the best-looking missus and whether long hair looks girly.

Whilst the Dutch may prepare for the tournament through pointless recrimination and petty squabbling, when they finally step out onto the pitch they are likely to be a big threat. If Ruud Van Nistelrooy plays, his performance in Portugal will be as important as it is in the English Premiership and you wouldn't bet against a renewed battle with Thierry Henry settling this title either. But that's if Ruud can keep at bay not only the competing claims of fellow strikers of exceptional talent (Makaay, Hasselbaink, Kluivert, Van Hooijdonkey etc) but also if he is still talking to them, and/or if the coach is prepared to pick him with certain others who don't like him etc.

Looking to the future, young Wesley Sneijder will barely be out of his teens by the time the group stages finish. However he has already made a huge impact with Ajax. Like Matthew Le Tissier at Southampton his 'apprenticeship' in the reserves at Ajax was virtually non-existent as he was catapulted into the first team and instantly impressed with his vision. Like the great Saints deity he is also both footed. Of course, this being Holland and not (pre-Sven) England he was quickly playing also for the national team and could emerge in the six months prior to the tournament as the cog which really gets Holland going after they laboured to a 6-1 aggregate play-off victory against Scotland.

Apart from the household names in the squad you could also look out for Andy Van der Meyde and the amusing pronunciation possibilities of Rafael Van Der Vaart and Andre Ooijer. All the others are household names from Van der Sar, through Cocu, Davids, Seedorf, Stam, de Boer etc. If Relate can get involved, or perhaps even Boutros Boutros Ghali, who knows what may be achieved.

Coach: Dick Advocaat

 ## Very Quick Quiz

Which of the following helps to explain the vicious in-fighting which has characterised the Dutch national football team over the years?

a) relaxed drug laws (contrary to right-wingers' arguments in Britain, this has not led to the falling apart of society, but often a more balanced attitude to drugs, in the context of a much healthier society than we have in Britain)

b) relaxed attitudes to sex (contrary to right-wingers' arguments in Britain, this has not led to raging immorality, but a more responsible attitude to sex amongst the young, in the context of a much lower teenage pregnancy rate than we have in Britain)

c) relaxed licensing laws (contrary to right-wingers' arguments in Britain, this does not mean a permanently drunk population, but a more responsible attitude to drinking, in the context of an enjoyable cafe society)

d) serious environmental legislation (contrary to right-

wingers' arguments in Britain, this greater concern for
the environment has not damaged the Dutch economy which is still much richer [per person] than ours
in Britain)

e) enhanced social benefits (which though not at the
levels of Scandinavia still provide the population with
a better safety net than we do in Britain for our vulnerable sectors of society)

Italy

Christian Vieri

Although the same could be true to a lesser extent of Filippo Inzaghi, rarely have I been so perplexed by the Vieri
hype one minute, just to see it fully justified the next.
The man clearly has the ability to be awesome. If his pace
and power are put to good effect as he nears his 31st
birthday, Vieri could bow out of international football
on a high. As ever the Italians will look good on paper,
and better in the shirts (as long as you ignore the hair)
but the organised defending and pretty pretty passing
must come to something. Vieri is (possibly) the man,
although at the moment he is sulking his way through
matches for Internazionale, apparently I am told because
he wants to leave. One might be inclined to think he's an
ungrateful rich b*******?

As with the Premiership and Ruud Van Nistelrooy, it is
no surprise to learn that last season's player of the year
was a foreigner in Pavel Nedved. However, one player
who has recently emerged is Perugia's Fabrizio Miccoli.
So good that he is now Juventus' Fabrizio Miccoli, he has
broken though into the Azzurri squad at just the right

time after some eye-catching performances. Rumours that previous elevation to the national squad were thwarted by his refusal to wear a silly shoulder length wig like the rest of the team are, of course, absolute twaddle which I just made up.

Coach: Giovanni Trapattoni

 ## Very Quick Quiz

Azzurri means which of the following:

    a) Blues   b) Boys   c) Girls   d) Diving Cheats
   e) One of the most over-rated teams in the world,
although I'll feel really embarassed about this if they
manage to win

Latvia

Perhaps Miholaps, perhaps Pahars, but very definitely Verpakovskis

Wow, Latvia seems to have a wealth of attacking talent that no-one has ever heard of. In last season's Latvian championship (2002), Mihail Milohaps won the Latvian golden boot award for a second successive season. Overall he scored a goal a game for Latvian giants Skonto Riga and earned a move to the Russian league for 2003, although like Pahars' move to Southampton he had to settle for a less fashionable club in Spartak-Alaniya. However at international level he has struggled to just a couple of goals at around one every ten games.

For a long time, the goal-scoring responsibilities for Latvia lay on the diminutive shoulders of the little Latvian himself, Marian Pahars. Known as the Latvian

Michael Owen, he certainly made the grade at Premier-ship level after his move from Skonto Riga, taking some of the 'Saints are staying up' duties away from Le Tissier as his powers faded in the late 1990s. However, as Southampton reached the cup final, Pahars moved from one operation to the next, his only real impact on the season being an outrageous dive to take three unde-served points from Everton. At present, rumours of his recovery are much exaggerated or at least each comeback appearance seems to end in a new injury or recurrence of an old one. Him and Agustin Delgado are currently in negotiations to write an article for *The Lancet*, the British medical journal. If he is fit, Latvia will have an attack capable of scoring goals. (At the time of writing Pahars did appear in a Southampton shirt again, looking lively for the last 25 minutes of a 1-0 defeat at Aston Villa. He also played the last two minutes for Latvia against Turkey in the play-off second leg. What the point of that was I'm not sure, but he didn't get injured at least!)

With the inability of Milohaps to click with the national team and Pahars injuries we have seen the rapid emergence of yet another Skonto Riga player, Maris Ver-pakovskis. Verpakovskis will no doubt be mispro-nounced by the so-called experts wheeled out on television, at least unless he does enough to impress them. Turkish commentators already know his name as he scored the only goal of the home leg and one of the Latvia pair in a 2-2 draw as Latvia pleasingly and surpris-ingly proved that serious surprises are really still possible in international football by winning their play-off against 'third at the World Cup' Turkey. Verpakovskis looks quick and with an eye for goal. Latvian television are calling Michael Owen the old Maris Verpakovskis. Beware.

Verpakovskis finds himself emerging for Latvia in his mid twenties. However, Igor Semjonovs (the Latvian Wayne Rooney?) will not yet be 19 by the time of the tournament. That said, he has emerged as a powerful force in the – you guessed it – Skonto Riga midfield and has already been thrown into the national team. Apart from these players, Latvia doesn't look like it ought to produce surprises, but the continuing ability of players (eg Kolinko) to perform beyond their club form will be crucial for what is likely to become everyone's second team of the tournament.

Coach: Aleksandr Starkovs

 Very Quick Quiz

Which of the following is not a Latvian top division team who normally trail in after Skonto Riga, who win the title?

a) Ventspils   b) Metalurgs   c) Dinaburg

d) Valmeira   e) PFK/Daugava

Portugal

The Crowd

Though the 'golden generation' of Portuguese football is felt to have disappointed, the last few years have actually exceeded anything that came before for Portugal in terms of tournament qualification. This time, the remnants of the golden generation have the chance to mix with younger blood and at home too. The talent is undoubted: Figo, Couto, Pauleta, Conceicao, Joao Pinto, Baia not to mention the well hidden potential of Postiga and Boa Morte. There is no doubt this lot can beat the best in the world. In preparation they drew in England and Holland and beat Brazil. As well as the best in the world they also beat Scotland at home. So, much will depend on whether the crowds back them to the hilt, or turn fickle when the chips are down. One suspects that patience is wearing thin amongst the public, so Portugal need to get off to a good start and keep the momentum going; then – like the French public didn't know what football was before 1998 but ended up playing a big part in the success – they may gain the confidence to go on and win it.

Cultural differences are important and should not be mocked, and I can understand, for instance, why the Koreans say the second name before the first name. There's a kind of logic to it which might even be more sensible than the way we do it. But why oh why oh why do Brazilians have just one name? Anyway, one such Brazilian – now naturalised Portuguese – is Deco. He was player of the season in 2002/03 in which Porto cruised the league, sneaked the cup and broke Celtic hearts in the UEFA Cup (much better to have taken a first round fall and saved your money boys!). In that same season Cristiano Ronaldo presumbly did something he no longer does if he was to become one of the hottest properties in Europe. Still, he is still pretty young and perhaps he will perform in a Portugal shirt (what is known as the Smicer effect). Much the same might be said of Helder Posterior.

Coach: Luiz Felipe Scolari

Very Quick Quiz

If Helder Postiga were not setting the footballing world alight at Tottenham Hotspur, what would he most likely be doing instead?

 a) Reading   b) Listening to music   c) Accountancy
d) A degree in fine art   e) Fishing

Russia

The Agony of No Choice

Is it just me or do the efficient and dour Soviet teams seem even more so in the current Russian guise? Looking down the list of players one struggles to pick out a name which will set Portugal 2004 alight. Defender Onopko? Forward Beschastnykh? Midfielder Karpin? Henry the mild-mannered janitor? Could be! Actually those players have over 250 caps and 50 international goals between them, but really I'd probably bet more money on Hong Kong Phooey setting the European Championships alight.

Leaving aside such cynicism, one name to emerge recently in domestic soccer is Tajikistan-born Dmitri Loskov. He scored the decisive goal as Lokomotiv Moscow beat CSKA Moscow in the play-off match to decide the 2002 title and finally made the national team aged 26. Despite previous coaches preferring Alexander Mostovoi, he undoubtedly has talent. An attacking midfielder, Loskovc has the potential to make a big impact in his first major championships, aged 30. For Russia so far he has not always done well, but the adjustment from club football where he has been a central figure may help to explain that.

Breaking into the Russian team at around the same time as Loskov was Rotor Volgagrad's Evgeni Aldonin; at 24 he should have a few more major championships before him although as a defender – albeit a bit more of a threat than Claus Lundekvam – he may not have the same potential to become a name as result of the tournament.

Finally, we must forget Alexei Smertin. A player so good and of such proven international class that Roman Abramovich is said to have signed him for Chelsea from Bordeaux as a favour to a business associate (strictly above board all that post-Soviet business dealing right?) but only once they'd found another club mug enough to take him on loan. That club was Portsmouth FC, meaning by default that Smertin is not good enough to have a big impact on Euro 2004.

Coach: Georgi Yartsev

 ## A Very Quick Quiz

Arch 'Ruskie' of the Cold War, Stalin was in fact from which Soviet republic?

      a) Tajikistan   b) Belarus   c) Georgia
             d) Latvia   e) Estonia

Spain

Raul, Finally? Or Will Reyes be King of Kings?

We can, if we want, rabbit on about 30 years (and rising) of hurt and all that, but imagine being a Spanish football supporter. Chances are you may have stronger local allegiances in the first place, but in any case, watching your team under-perform must have been cruel torture year after year. And imagine that in 1966, if instead of England winning the thing we had struggled to a 1-1 draw with Honduras and lost 1-0 at home to Northern Ireland before limply getting eliminated. So what hope this time for Spain who did just this in 1982? Which of the big names might finally remember to produce the performance the stage demands?

Well it seems almost silly to talk about the established stars. We all know they are capable of almost anything, including losing 1-0 at home to Greece and making probably the most spectacular cock-up ever by a team playing in a major championships as hosts. So let us forget the superstars of Spanish football of the past and talk instead of Jose Antonio Reyes. I don't know if you remember, but back in late 2003 the Real Madrid coach Carlos Quieros – after extensive lessons on being irritating from Alex Ferguson whilst at Man U – responded to suggestions that Real Madrid needed a top quality defender by saying that his team of superstars did not need defenders because they attacked and therefore did not need to defend. Do you remember that?

Well, the next game was against Sevilla. After about 30 minutes the score was Sevilla 4-0 Real Madrid with the home team ultimately cruising to a 4-1 victory. By that time Madrid had withdrawn a young defender – I forget his name – whose performance had been so similar to the rest of the 'defence' that he was made a scapegoat. He sat on the bench sobbing. I sent him a video of Scott Marshall – allegedly decribed by Francis Benali as the worst player he'd ever seen – to cheer him up a bit. I must send Francis a video of himself. In any case, in that spell where Sevilla went 4-0 up, it was not simply the quality of Madrid's defending which was their downfall, but that Jose Antonio Reyes absolutely took them apart.

World Soccer recently described the 20-year-old as a 'fantasy footballer', and certainly he looks to have pace, skill and vision in abundance. Like others with such talent he seems occasionally to exasperate his manager, although he must be pleased to have such a quality player in a team (Sevilla) renowned for no-nonsense toughness and hard tackling. Reyes has recently been promoted to the Spanish national team. He seems full of confidence, and with the play-offs out of the way, maybe he is the player that can encourage Spain finally to fulfil their potential.

Coach: Inaki Saez

 Very Quick Quiz

Which is the nastiest 'derby' game in the world?
        a) Lazio-Roma   b) Southampton-Portsmouth
   c) River-Boca   d) Betis-Sevilla   e) Blackburn-Burnley

Sweden

Anders Svensson

Talking of patience wearing thin (as in Spanish fans and their team)...come on Anders...what's it all about eh? You bang in the free-kicks versus Argentina, you almost win the game with a golden goal against Senegal with the most fantastic drag back and shot. Every time I look at a Swedish score you seem to have scored or been involved and you're averaging a goal every four games from midfield. And yet put you in a Saints shirt! You need an extra touch, you don't seem to put your foot in and you score one goal every eight games (and rising). Come on man! You look lazy and lethargic and the fact that you were supposed to be the creative replacement for Le Tiss is no excuse. Sort it out! Go and wow them in Portugal and then come back and start knocking them in for the Saints (although if his form gets any lower I wouldn't bank on him being with the Saints by then). The other Svensson from Southampton might also be important.

Worth mentioning in amongst all the Svenssons, Anderssons and such like are Niklas Skoog and Dick Last. No idea what their football is like (Last has only one cap) but great names. Actually Skoog has four goals in four games though all against Qatar and North Korea so don't hold your breath any.

To be taken more seriously, as any sportsman called Kim really should be, is Kim Kallstrom, one important reason why Djurgardens won the Swedish league in 2002 (a title they retained in 2003). A strong two-footed mid-fielder who gets his fair share of goals...hey, maybe they'd swap him for Anders. Kallstrom is only young so could emerge at Portugal 2004. Alexander Farnerud is a couple of years younger than Kallstrom but is already a target of many clubs. He has already played for and scored for the national team.

Coaches: The very wonderfully named Lars Lagerback and Tommy Soderberg.

 ## Very Quick Quiz

Which is the funniest joke?

a) The Swedish chemist sketch in which the man wants to buy a deodorant and for which the punchline is 'Neither, I want it for my armpits'.
b) The joke about why does a dog lick its balls told in Norwegian.
c) The joke about why no one goes hungry in the desert.

Switzerland

Alexander Frei

Alexander Frei is 24 years old and plays in Rennes with the Czech goalie chap (Cech)...at least at the time of writing. Frei is scoring a goal every one and a half games for Switzerland and will need to take the majority of chances coming his way if they are to produce any surprises this time. Let's face it the Swiss will need something. This is not to under-estimate a side which drew with the hosts in both World Cup USA 94 and Euro 96 but, and this is a big but (as the Archbishop of Canterbury said to the Duchess of York) something really special will need to emerge for them.

In this sense, one wonders if the European Under-17 Championship-winning team of 2002 offers any promise for the Swiss. Yes and no. Of course by 2006, 2008 and 2010 this group of players may have produced several fine players for the Swiss national team. However, in the short term the best of those players is Phillippe Senderos. The 'however' in that last sentence says nothing about my feelings concerning Senderos' obvious potential and everything about the fact that he is a defender which may not be where Switzerland need the talent to emerge. Furthermore, it is by no means certain that at just 17 young Phillippe has time in any case to break into the national team by the summer of 2004.

Coach: Kobi Kuhn

 ## Very Quick Quiz

Several languages, cuckoo clocks, mountains, cheese full of holes, expensive everything, yodelling, refusal to join the UN, let alone the EU. How are we to characterise the Swiss?

a) Odd   b) Distinctly odd   c) Strange

d) Very strange   e) Barking

Answers

Bulgaria
e) Letchkov. I finally remembered it but I'm still not sure of the first name or the spelling!

Croatia
The word to change is banana and the order is a, e, c, b and d. With apologies

Czech Republic
Possibly all except d)

Denmark
e) Lee Carsley

England
All of the above

France
c) Kenya, as a former British colony. Also, I don't know, because that would take more research than I've got time for, but as rugby playing country, it is also entirely likely that Toulouse does not provide the birth place for any of France's current football squad

Germany
1: a) 13, b) 45, c)48, d) 66, e) 74
2: 6, the only one that Germany scored in)

Greece
e) and let's be fair [and perhaps not as spectacularly as Turkey] Greek football has improved a lot in recent years. I'd certainly bet on them to beat Scotland these days. Despite my harsh words they could yet make me eat humble 'cheese' pie

Holland
Who can say? It's all a bit of a mystery really, isn't it?

Italy
The answer is, of course, 'Blues'

Latvia
e) who withdrew because of financial difficulties

Portugal
e) because his father Manuel is a fisherman working out of the Portuguese port of Varzim for whom young Helder played initially

Russia
c) Georgia

Spain
Having only experienced one of them I really can't say, but the Seville derby is renowned for its passion. Betis president Manuel Ruiz de Lopera recently forbade his players from 'fraternising' with any of Sevilla's for instance.

Sweden
c) with the totally amusing punchline being: 'Because of all the sandwiches there'...sand which is there...geddit?

Switzerland
Yes

Portuguese Culture & Football Stadia

In this chapter you'll get a bit of flavour of Portuguese life, with the handy phrases section as promised at the end. I've never been to Portugal so can't say from experience, but it is a popular holiday destination, and visitors who stray from the beaten track and try to discover the 'real' Portugal are invariably rewarded by getting lost...er, no sorry I mean by beautiful countryside, charming hidden restaurants etc. Using some old guidebooks I aim to give you a flavour of all aspects of Portuguese life from the cuisine to the currency – the escudo.[34] So before you can say, 'that'll be three million pesetas please', here we go...starting with the business end – where the footy gets played and moving through culture, history etc.

The Stadia

Of the 10 stadia which will be used in the finals, seven have the minimum capacity of 30,000. Only the Dragao in Oporto and the Jose Alvalade (52,000) and Da Luz (where the final will be held on 4 July, 65,000) in Lisbon hold more. Of the others, simply to hear the names is to conjure up the most wonderful images of Latin life. At Braga, there's the impressive Municipal stadium for instance. Meanwhile at Aveiro, there's the unforgettably named 'Municipal stadium'. And at Coimbra, of course, there's the charmingly named Municipal stadium. Municipal is of course Portuguese for 'Municipal'. Simply to hear the names inspires such awe and eager anticipation.

Portugal has invested nearly £300 million in hosting the tournament, including 10 stadia of which seven will have been built from scratch. As outsiders to host the tournament in the first place, many suggested that Portugal would not be up to the task (predicting chaos and incompetence in organisation) and domestically the suggestion has been that the money would have been better spent on helping resolve social problems and that the expense will place even further burdens on an already creaking Portuguese economy. Of course the hope is that in return for a considerable investment, tourism will massively increase, thus partially or even wholly paying

34 Joke. I know it's changed now.

for the tournament and attracting to Portugal people who may never have been before but might subsequently revisit, such as the author. Also, the venues have attracted more Portuguese fans for the current season.

Alphabetical Listing of the Venues

Aveiro
There will be just two group matches at this stadium especially built for the tournament. It holds 30,000 fans and the team Beira Mar. It is one of the stadia with the magical 'Municipal' label.

Braga
Like the Municipal at Aveiro, this is a newly constructed stadium for 30,000 fans which will host two group games and is called Estadio Municipal. The home team is called Sporting Braga. I'm sure 'braga' in Spanish has something to do with ladies underwear, although that is relevant here for God only knows what reason.[35]

Coimbra
This is one of the 'remodelled' stadia, in Portugal's former historic capital extending to 30,000 the capacity for home team Academica. Again the stadium is a municipal one and again two group games will take place here.

Faro-Loulé
A brand new stadium on the Algarve with lovely wave-like patterns on the seats. It will host two group matches and one quarter-final. Called the Estadio Algarve.

35 Google translation tells me it's 'panties'.

Guimarães

The attractive Estadio Afonso Henriques has been remodelled to hold the minimum required 30,000. Normally playing here are Vitoria Guimarães, the sort of team that serious 'anoraks' have heard of but not normal people. There will be two group matches here.

Leiria

Not for Leiria the Municipal tag. No the home stadium for Uniao Leiria – which will host two group matches – is called Dr Magalhaes Pessoa. Capacity has been increased from a modest 11,000 to 30,000.

Lisbon (Benfica)

A brand new Estadio da Luz has been built next to the old one, and the remarkable space-age construction holds 65,000. Benfica's ground is going to host five matches in total including the final. The stadium has the technology to go with the space-age look. Behind each goal are a couple of dozen internet connections allowing pictures to be relayed instantly. There are 1,000 press places and over 100 commentary positions.

Lisbon (Sporting)

The new Estadio José Alvalade has a capacity of 52,000 which Sporting are now half-filling on a regular basis as Portuguese fans begin to get enthusiastic about the championships. The old Estadio José Alvalade (next door) was getting average crowds of less than 10,000. Three group games, a quarter and a semi-final will be here.

Oporto (FC Porto)

Like the Lisbon variety, the new Estadio Dragao has been thrown up next to the old Estadio das Antas. Like the Estadio José Alvalade it holds 52,000 spectators. The home of FC Porto it will host the tournament's opening game, two other group matches, a quarter-final and a semi-final. Estadio Dragao probably means Dragon Stadium. Estadio das Antas is less likely to mean Stadium of Ants but you never can tell!

Oporto (Boavista)

The Estadio do Bessa has been rebuilt for the championships with several extra seating sections. The home of Boavista will host three group matches and holds, like all but three of the tournament stadia, 30,000 spectators.

History

Throwing it All Away

One of the oldest and most powerful countries in Europe (well established by 1200), Portugal forgot to keep up in the 19th and 20th centuries and has found itself playing catch-up ever since. Unlike other former dominant powers such as Holland and Spain it has rather thrown it all away. On the other hand Portugal's 'backwardness' (I hate to use the word – it conjures up unnecessary prejudices) and shall we say 'out of the way-ness' has been very helpful in terms of its ability to stay out of wars. However it did decide to pitch in with the Allies in 1916, leaving it financially depleted, short of manpower and in chaos.

Whilst Lisbon and Oporto might seem relatively normal big cities, with all the associated grime as well as glamour, go a few kilometres outside and you are travelling to a different world and a different time. A history lesson in itself. So if you get the chance to travel outside the major cities and resorts then do so; however expect to get stared at – especially if you are other than Portuguese and white. Oh and for heaven's sake don't drive! Hiring a car can be the ideal way to see a country quickly, but in some places such as Romania and Portugal, it just isn't worth it. Everyone drives like loonies and Portugal heads the road deaths per million of population stats, certainly for the EU and possibly the world.

In terms of history, Portugal emerged as an independent kingdom in the 12th century. According to myth, Odysseus founded Lisbon on his way home from Troy. There is also loads of stuff I could include about invasions and royal dynasties but I'm guessing you're not really interested in all that kind of stuff? Call me a mindreader. Let me give you a flavour in the form of a few chronologically ordered sentences which will very possibly be quite useless to you. All you need to do however is throw in a few King Afonsos and Queen Isabellas and you should be able to bluff your way through after dinner discussions on Portuguese history. That'll save you reading a few books, eh? (All of the following are from Richard Robinson writing in the 1988 *Blue Guide*.)

> 'The [Iberian] peninsula as a whole passed from Carthaginian to Roman domination as a result of the Second Punic War (218-202 BC)...Lisbon was Julius Caeser's capital in 60 BC.' (p.13)

> 'With the demise of the [Roman] Empire the peninsula was invaded after 409 [AD] by four groups of "barbarians", all from beyond the Pyrenees [including]... the Vandals...[and] Visigoths.' (p.14)

Muslim forces then invaded from North Africa...

'The Christian reconquest may be said to have commenced in 718 with Palayo's symbolic "victory" over a small force of Moors at Covadonga, in the Asturias.' (p.15)

'Complete independence...was formally recognised by Pope Alexander III in 1179 [and] the new kingdom had a population estimated at 400,000.' (pp.15-16)

'The country was ravaged by the "Black Death" during the reign of Afonso IV (1325-57) which decimated the population in 1348-49. In 1355 took place the murder of Ines de Castro (the Galician mistress of the Infante Pedro), whose family was suspected of furthering Castillian [Spanish] interests.' (yadda yadda yadda – just like EastEnders really) (p.17)

But even *EastEnders* doesn't get quite this silly...1373.

'Portugal was at this time allied with John of Gaunt, Duke of Lancaster, who...claimed the Castillian throne (for both he and Edmund, Earl of Cambridge had married daughters of Pedro the Cruel)...[King] Fernando [of Portugal] started negotiations, promising Beatriz, his ten-year-old heiress, to Edward, six-year-old son of Edmund of Cambridge.' (p.17)

Actually it's more like *Blackadder*. Let's skip a few years eh, and see how they're getting on...ooh look, they've taken over the world!

'After Papal arbitration, Spain and Portugal divided the world at the Treaty of Tordesillas (1494) at a line 370 leagues west of Cape Verdes. Manuel I (1495-1521) and Joao III (1521-57) promoted such expansion as part of a royal enterprise, the Crown taking its "royal fifth" of the trading profits.' (p.20)

'The late 15th and 16th centuries witnessed a flowering of the arts and literature...Printing was introduced in c 1487 and there were many contacts with the humanism of the Renaissance.' (p.21)

'With a view to balancing trade as Brazilian sugar lost its

markets, the famous Methuen treaty of December 1703 was signed...England admitted Portuguese wines on preferential terms.' (p.23)

In the year following the treaty, and to celebrate its success, a special festival was held in Lisbon. An area of town was lit up at night and a game involving an inflated pig's bladder took place between English sailors and the locals. Thus it came to pass that in the 'Stadium of Light' England beat the locals on 4 July 1704 in the first football match played in Portugal. Spookily, almost exactly 300 years ago.[36] England won 3-0 with goals from The Earl of Beckham, Owen of Lancaster and a burly Irish galley boy called Patrick O'Rooney.

OK, let's get through the rest of this sharpish:

'On 1 November 1755 Lisbon was convulsed by an earthquake...The reign of Maria I united material progress and political conservatism [Napoleonic era]...In 1823 a rural reaction against liberal constituionalism began...The infrastructure of improved communications and the investment of foreign capital allowed a general expansion of the economy from the 1870s. Nevertheless, Portugal lagged behind the rest of western Europe...By 1900 a quarter of Portugal's trade and industry was foreign-controlled, and one sixth of industry was foreign-owned, half of this being in British hands.' (pp.23-29)

Wow, and to think Charles Clarke thinks this isn't worthwhile!

OK, I think Richard Robinson has taken us as far as the limits of copyright law and your patience will stretch. Before moving on, let me just emphasise that Charles Clarke's views on education are idiotic. History not only

---

36 This is just in case anyone thinks I've not made this up! Although the fascinating treaty bit is true!

has intrinsic value (except as abbreviated by me) but is the ideal media for helping students acquire a whole range of practical, personal and research skills which will serve them well in future life. Much the same can be said of subjects such as Geography, International Relations and Heritage, all of which can be studied in the excellent Department of International Studies at the excellent Nottingham Trent University in the excellent city of Nottingham. That's my day job. Could I just say hello to Roy, Chris, Evan, Ronan, Ces and anybody else that knows me...

Back to the action. A little commentary on contemporary Portuguese history may be more useful to the traveller for setting the beauty and the poverty you will experience in context. Despite Portugal's rich history it had fallen so far behind that even rapid growth throughout the 1950s and 1960s (9%) failed to pull Portugal off the bottom of the European economic league table by 1980. Some of the growth was swallowed up by population growth which has more than doubled since 1900. Increases in welfare provision were swallowed up by inflation. Struggles in overseas colonies were expensive and demoralised the armed forces.

In 1974 a virtually bloodless coup took place and in the now so-called Flower Revolution, soldiers marched through Lisbon with red carnations sticking out of their ends. *[Editor's note: We believe he means 'ends of their rifles'.]* Initially and unsurprisingly given social problems, the communists held considerable influence but over time a more stable coalition emerged around the centre and Portugal took its place in the European Union. The End.

As outsiders it was a particular coup for Portugal to get this tournament. The visitor from England should be prepared for something different. The contrast between colonial splendour and stark urban poverty is great. Though it is unlikely to happen, English fans should show a level of restraint and sensitivity that they have not done in the past. Be nice to the police and they will be charming and friendly, but don't f*** about. Similarly, there are areas of Lisbon that you just don't want to treat with carelessness, where violence is a way of life – and that's just the Brazilian prostitutes. But now we are straying onto the realm of 'culture' or at least of advice for the traveller so there we finish our whirlwind, superficial, predominantly useless squiz at Portuguese history.

Culture

Well I say culture, but that's not really, actually what I mean, is it? I mean there are just tonnes of palaces, churches, museums, gardens and narrow streets and you get a depressingly brief review of these in the section on Lisbon (on the grounds that if you're going you'll buy a guide book right?). Outside Lisbon, life is completely different and that is covered in the section on 'off the beaten track.' But let's face it, you're likely to be in a pretty big town or city waiting for a football match and what you really want to know under culture is 'what's it like?' What new stuff to try and eat, how the night-life differs and how strong the beer is etc. On that basis, I proceed!

Well at that time of year you should be dining al fresco and at least in Lisbon enjoying breezes to pleasantly take the edge off the heat. Of course this being on the Atlantic it could rain at any time. The major cities are highly cosmopolitan and offer a mixture of cuisines not only from around the world, but also bringing together the specialities of Portugal. As rough translations for different types of establishment the following may help:

A *tasca* is a local intimate tavern type place

A *cervejara* is more of a beer hall with late opening and snacks

A *casa de pasto* is a three-course budget set menu type of place

A *marisquiera* is a fish dish place and

A *churrasqueira* roasts meat on a spit, something which has arrived from Brazil

Vegetarians had better head for ethnic restaurants, rationalise the eating of fish for a few days or be content with salad. Things to try if you're one of those people who wants to do the authentic bit are:

Bacalhau – salted, dried cod

Caldo Verde – a type of soup, described in guides as 'Kale' soup

Porco a alentejana – pork in port

[Editor's note: We found evidence of drooling on the manuscript at this point]

Frango a piri-piri – Barbequed chilli chicken *[Ditto]*

Portugal is of course famous for port and madeira but other wines have been rapidly improving and you may wish to try the local cherry brandy, particularly if you are a fan of cherries, brandy or cherry brandy.

In 1994, Lisbon was European Capital of Culture. This is an odd concept. Prior to Lisbon it had been Antwerp (a fantastic city for beer, chips and mussels) and Glasgow. But perhaps Lisbon is culture in a more stereotypical sense with plenty of opportunities to enjoy not only the endless museums and churches (see below under Lisbon) but also classical music as well as jazz and other musical forms. After the fall of the dictatorship in 1974 Portugal has become home to many from former colonies such as Mozambique, Angola, Guinea Bissau and Brazil and many of these influences have been absorbed into local musical styles.

Lisbon, and with subtle regional variations Portugal, also has a thing called *fado* loosely translated as 'fate' which is a musical style which deals with the concept of longing for that which is lost or never attained (sounds a bit wet to me!). In any case *fado* is thus intense, melancholic and moody and presumably has heavily influenced Luis Figo's diving style. If that doesn't sound like your kind of scene (and there are many bars offering the acoustic guitar, 12-string mandolin music) there are plenty of other clubs in Bairro Alto most particularly and a bit of a dance scene in Rato. Films are generally sub-titled rather than dubbed. Plenty of people expect tips, including toilet attendants, at more or less the English norm of 10%.

Advice for the Traveller

Off the Beaten Track

Driving is not easy in Portugal so if you are getting off the beaten track then you may want to think carefully about the best way to do it. Personally I would suggest the approach of thinking 'sod it, there's too much football on TV' and therefore staying in a bar. For the slightly more adventurous there are actually enough nice things to do for instance near to Lisbon (Sintra – World Heritage Site, Queluz – Rococo architecture and the resorts of Estoril and Cascais) and in Oporto drinking yourself into a port-soaked stupor.

But beyond that Portugal is just an amazing place. The pictures are just wild, desolate country and fine colonial buildings. Here, for those who may be lucky enough to be watching matches in Braga, Coimbra or Faro-Loulé here is a little on each.

Braga

The ancient town of Braga is easily reached from Porto and is Portugal's third most important city. It is a busy industrial city which produces leather goods, textiles and bricks among others. It has many sporting facilities and bars/clubs. Nick Timmons intriguingly describes it as 'rather reminiscent of London in the sixties' (see bibliography). Its centre has an enormous concentration of historical buildings and churches such that it has been known as 'Portuguese Rome'.

Coimbra

Famous for having Portugal's first University founded in around 1290. The students still maintain many of the ancient customs including composing the *fado* songs (see elsewhere in this chapter) which are mercifully less melancholic than those of Lisbon and which may be heard in the towns many small bars. The main 16th century buildings of the University are on the hill overlooking the town arranged around a large and impressive courtyard overlooked by a clock tower nicknamed for some reason 'the goat'.

Faro-Loulé

Loulé is an attractive market town; all white-washed houses, drinking fountains and castle walls. Loads of local craftsmen, charming markets etc. You really want to go when it's not full of football supporters, don't you? Naturally, Loulé has its fair share of attractive churches.

Advice for the Traveller
Lisbon

Many will fly to Lisbon and it's a fantastic city. Let's hope some of you are there for England's win in the final, but in any case, it is a city worth mentioning in some detail as an extraordinary mix. It has been described as the last city of the old world and the first of the new, whatever that might mean! Although now a huge city with many sprawling slums most of what will be of interest to you is concentrated in four main areas: Baixa/Alfama, Bairro Alto/Estrela, North Lisbon and Belem.

Baixa/Alfama

The Praca do Comercio is a focal point for Portugal's history being the site of the Royal Palace destroyed in 1755. Rebuilt as the palatial centre-piece of the city it is now home to much government administration, but still looks pretty palatial. Off the Praca do Comercio are all sorts of impressive buildings and avenues, but let's face it, you're going to buy a proper guide-book aren't you?

What you need to know is that there's loads of 'stuff'. The Rua Augusta entrance for instance leads to a network of Roman tunnels, galleries and baths. The Museu do Chiado has a great range of art dating from 1850 to 1950. The main market is the Mercado do Rebeira near the Elevador da Bica. In addition to that you've got somewhere in the region of a billion churches and half a billion museums.

Bairro Alto/Estrela

Here you will be able to get lost in the narrow winding streets of Santa Catarina which takes its name from the Igreja de Santa Catarina, another building which fell victim, along with maybe 40,000 people, to that earthquake of 1755. In this area too you'll find the Mercado 24 de Julho (which is a food and flower market) and the Jardim Botanico which occupies 10 acres of ground owned by the University's Science Faculty. With the dissolution of religious orders in 1834 the Palacio de Sao Bento became the Palacio de Assembleia Nacional, in other words the home of the national assembly, also in this locale. Museums, galleries, chuches, gardens and so on and so forth.

North Lisbon

Prior to Euro 2004 and subsequent to the association of travel agencies congress of 1994, Portugal was host to the EXPO 98 malarky, celebrating the 500th anniversary of Vasco de Gama's first voyage to India. The theme of the 'Expo' was thus the sea, part of which was the Oceanario de Lisboa which is now a permanent aquarium and the second largest in the world. Parque Eduardo VII is actually named after King Edward VII after he visited Portugal in 1903 to add a bit of zip to the Anglo-Portuguese alliance first negotiated in 1386. Queenie herself (you know the gracious one) arrived in 1957 and they added a couple of pillars in her honour. Hey and guess what, there are more museums (including the modern art one if you like that sort of thing; looks like splodges to me), palaces and, er, museums (that's a relief then).

Belem

I am told, although in pictures it looks just like so many other buildings, the Tower of Belem symbolises Portugal's noble (questionable as in the case of all imperial powers) past as an imperial power. The Tower was commissioned by Manuel I and built between 1515 and 1521. In my book it says it was built by the architect Fransisco de Arruda but I think they meant he swanned around in a comfy tunic barking out the orders rather than actually doing the donkey work. Anyway, spectacular it is, so go and see. The usual monuments including the Padrao dos Descobriemtos facing the River Tejo at the Belem water-front. And there's a cultural centre and a planetarium. Belem also has an aquarium a little to the west called the Aquario Vasco de Gama, which opened in 1898.

Top Ten Tips

Don't drive. The taxis are cheap. They might drive like loonies but they know what they're doing (you don't) and they'll charge you bugger all relative to what you'd pay in the UK.

Don't jump in the river. Don't throw anyone else in the river. Those fish got big by eating sh*t from the sewerage outlet pipes – nice!

Think very carefully before employing the services of prostitutes. Dodgy parts of town, big friends, diseases. You know the kind of thing.

Change your drinking habits. Bars don't start ringing bells and closing. Pace yourself. Nothing but ill can be achieved by necking pints at 15-minute pace and calling anyone who fails to keep up a 'big jessie'.

English may not be as widely spoken as you would hope or would expect after being to other tourist destinations. So make sure your body language is friendly and that you treat people with respect. (Sorry to patronise you!)

Take sun cream (d'oh!) and an umbrella.

Learn some Portuguese. Just the basics and not just from the incredibly helpful guide below! Portuguese looks pretty much like Spanish, but as the Dutch are not wild on German speakers so the Portuguese would prefer you to learn some of their language. If the person you are talking to speaks English it may be better struggle with their English than to impress them with your Spanish.

If you're in Lisbon and you've time, try and get yourself to Sintra. Sounds lovely and has been a UNESCO World Heritage Site since 1995. Famous for (wait for it): palaces and churches.

It is polite to address people as *Senhor* or *Senhora* (senyor/a)

The telephone country code for Portugal is 351.

Language

Of course any country, during a football championship or not, is likely to be much more enjoyable if you understand a bit of the lingo. So here is your handy phrase part of the book to enhance your enjoyment of Portugal 2004. As well as useful phrases, we've thrown in some useless ones too – just for novelty value. [Thanks to Ronan Fitzsimons for his language consultancy services and trademark sense of 'humour'.]

Key Vocabulary

One - *Um/uma* Two - *Dois/duas* Three - *Três*
Four - *Quatro* Five - *Cinco* Beer/s - *Cerveja/s*

In the Stadium

Continentals usually like to whistle or jump up and down during singing. If you would like to teach them some of our songs to jump and whistle to, here are a small selection.

- One two, one two three, one two three four, five – nil!
  Um dois, um dois três, um dois três quatro, cinco-zero!

- En-ger-land, En-ger-land, En-ger-land
  In-gla-te-rra, In-gla-te-rra, In-gla-te-rra.

- Who ate all the pies?
  Quem comeu todos os empadões?

- You're shit and you know you are.
  Vocês são uma merda, e sabem disso.
- Who are ya?
  Quem são vocês?

- The referee's a wanker.
  O árbitro é um punheteiro.

And for general terrace chit-chat...

- They've got a Stadium of Light in Sunderland, you know, but at least in Lisbon I can understand the locals.
  Há um Estádio da Luz em Sunderland, sabes, mas pelo menos em Lisboa compreendo os habitantes.

- We're not all hooligans you know.
  Não somos todos desordeiros, sabes?

- How's life in the Group of Death?
  Como vai a vida no Grupo da Morte?

- At least you haven't got a bloody millennium dome in your country.
  Pelo menos vocês não têm um maldito domo do milénio no vosso país.

In the Bar/Restaurant

Chances are the menu will be in comical English or you won't eat there anyway. So here are some more interesting things to say:

- Too many sardines give me hiccups, but that's part of my charm with the opposite sex.
  Muitas sardinhas dão-me soluços, mas isso faz parte do meu charme com o sexo oposto.
- I'm a Geordie, me. D'ya fancy a beer, pet?
  Eu sou de Newcastle, em Grã-Bretanha. Queres uma cerveja, amorzinho?

- I have a hangover the size of Coimbra
  Tenho uma ressaca do tamanho de Coimbra.

- Does this food contain the innards of any previously living creature?
  Esta comida contém as tripas duma criatura anteriormente viva?

For No Good Reason

Some phrases for no other reason than demonstrating your ability to quickly pick up foreign languages.

- Hello, John. Gotta new motor?
  Olá, João. Tens un novo carro?

- You have unusually long hair for a man of your age.
  Tens os cabelos muito longos para un homem da tua idade

- Blue dogs are not unusual in Birmingham, Alabama, I'm told.
  Ouvi dizer que os cães azuis não são insólitos em Birmingham, Alabama.

- Do you ever feel there's too much garlic in your food?
  Nunca te apercebestes que há demasiado alho na tua comida?

- I would usually prefer a slightly younger donkey than the one your aunt recently purchased.
  Normalmente preferiria um burro ligeiramente mais jovem do que aquele que a tua tia comprou recentemente.

And If You're Feeling Brave, Foolish or Both

Some phrases to cement your reputation as a complete loon...

- If I had a T shirt like that I think I'd wear a waistcoat.
  Se eu tivesse um t-shirt assim, penso que usaria um colete.

[For when faced with local *fado* music]
- This music's crap. Haven't you got any Stiff Little Fingers?
  Esta música é uma merda. Não têm nada dos Stiff Little Fingers?

- I'm not sure which of you is the ugliest but Barry Manilow has a more attractive nose than you all.
  Não sei qual de vós é o mais feio, mas Barry Manilow tem um nariz mais atraente do que todos vós.

- Oh yes, I used to go drinking with George W Bush and afterwards he liked me to pleasure him with my tongue.
  Pois sim, antes saía a beber com George W Bush, e depois ele gostava que eu lhe desse prazer com a lingua].

And if you're feeling even braver, some phrases without translation. Just see where they take you... (handy phonetic translations though, so that you can get a feel for this beautiful language...)
- Este campo está semeado de trigo, assim pois não podemos jogar aqui
  [est cam-poo shtah semmay-ah-doo d' tree-goo, ass-eeem poysh nayng poo-day-moosh djoo-gar a kee]

- Fiquei assombrado ao ouvir as notícias sobre a menina dos olhos verdes com a mesa de carvalho
  [fee-kay-ee ass-sum-brah-doo ow oo-veer ass noo-tee-see-

ass sob-reh ah men-nee-na doosh oll-yoosh vehr-desh com
ah may-sah d' kar-vall-yoo]

- Segundo a operação se tornar mais ou menos
  necessária, teremos que adaptar os nossos planos
  [say-goon-doo ah oh-peh-rah-saing s' toor-nahr mighsh oo
  may-noosh neh-sess-sah-ree-ah, teh-ray-moosh k' a-dap-
  tahr oos nohs-soos plan-noosh]

- Estou encharcado até os ossos, mas estou em crer que
  ele não me compreende
  [shtow en-char-kah-doo ah-tay oos oss-oosh, mass shtow
  emm crehr k' el-lay naing may coom-preynd]

- Dir-lho-ei outra vez: trá-lo-ás na semana que vem?
  [deer-loo-ey oo-trah vesh: trah-loo-ash nah s' mah-na k'
  vehm]

[Editor's note: use these last phrases entirely at your own risk.
No kidding; they could mean absolutely anything. The pub-
lisher accepts no responsibility at all for anything untoward
that may befall you, the reader, as a result of voicing these
phrases in crowded Lisbon bars.]

Bibliography

Lisbon for Less (Compact Guide), London: Metropolis International, 1999.

Evans, D, *Portugal* (Cadogan Guides), London: Cadogan Books, 1990.

Fogarty, P (ed), *The Berlitz Traveller's Guide: Portugal*, New York: Berlitz, 1993.

Robertson, I, *Blue Guide: Portugal* (Third edition), London: W W Norton, 1988.

Timmons, N, *Off the Beaten Track: Portugal*, Ashbourne: Moorland Publishing Company, 1992.

Predictions

Prediction 1

At the time of writing clubs are beginning to organise to demand compensation for the release of their players to play in the tournament. I guess this is somewhat inevitable. Football clubs are businesses and the players are their biggest assets. As things stand, clubs pay players wages over the summer, whilst those players play for their national teams at the tournament. At the moment representatives of Europe's elite clubs are talking to UEFA about the situation; whether it will affect the tournament or not, I am not sure. *[Editor's note: Not much of a prediction!]*

You can see why the clubs might not feel this right but to me it seems that football just isn't what it used to be. Teams at domestic level used to change only rarely and you could pronounce all the names. But now what's it like? So, just as my Granddad used to complain about games being called off just because it was a bit wet and goals being disallowed simply because the goalie had been charged to the ground and trampled on by a hefty centre-forward, my first prediction is that many people will talk about football not being what it used to be, whilst a whole new generation will collect Panini stickers blissfully unaware that in 20 years time, when football is played in four quarters of 15 minutes with a stopping clock, a sin-bin and rolling substitutions, they will be the ones that say it's not what it used to be. As Rik on 'The Young Ones' said when responding to the comment that 'things certainly have been different since these new fan-gled changes'...'well of course they have otherwise they wouldn't be changes you old git!'

Prediction

My second prediction is that people will take it all far too seriously. This seems inevitable yet sad, and yet at the same time what makes football fantastic. You are going through a terrible divorce or worried you are going to get the sack...but if you then go to the match, when you know that only a victory will save your team from relegation or get them to the Cup Final, you can't think of anything else. A win and you think 'sod the divorce' or 'I'll get another job', a defeat and you'd gladly trade your job (or spouse) to change what had just happened. And yet, it is worth remembering that there are larger things afoot. And in a book of irreverence and downright stupidity at times, I would like to take this argument right back to earth with a bump to tell you a little about the issue of landmines and a group which is trying to eradicate their use world-wide. Tread on a landmine and you would realise how unimportant football is. Tread on a landmine and you would never play football/walk/live again. How many mine-affected countries do well in the World Cup –indeed, how many qualify! (Answer: Virtually none).

Prediction 3

My third prediction then is that some people will want to skip the next section. It is about the scourge of land-mines and about a group – the International Demining Group – set up to do something about it. If you do not feel this will be of interest to you then please do skip to the section marked Prediction Four but actually this is something you should be interested in. This is an area where political will, training and money actually could make a difference. So...[37]

A landmine is a victim-operated trap. The concept of the victim-operated trap has been employed throughout history; not only as a weapon but also in more mundane forms such as shop doorbells, car and house burglar alarms and the snares used by hunters to catch animals. Throughout history, concealed pits with spikes at the bottom have been used both in hunting and in warfare. Usually in warfare they have been used as a defensive ploy to give an outnumbered defender an edge to com-pensate for a lack of numbers, what is known in military parlance today as a 'force multiplier' – and used in exactly the same way that the landmine is used today;

[37] Material for this section was kindly provided by Graeme Goldsworthy, head of the International Demining Group based in Amsterdam.

and used they still are today in huge numbers.

Landmines are cheap and easy to produce, costing on average two or three dollars such that for the price of the current Chelsea line up you could get 300-400 million mines (possibly many more by the time of publication)! They can be manufactured virtually anywhere – any developing country which has the capacity to manufacture items in cheap plastic or wood can manufacture APMs (anti-personnel mines) in their thousand. They do not require the infrastructure of a vast military industrial complex and do not require precision engineering. They are easier to manufacture than a rifle bullet, a hand grenade, a mortar round or an artillery shell and the last three of these types of ordnance can easily be converted into landmines with the simple expedient of an exchange of fuse mechanisms. So if you have the shells but not the artillery pieces to fire them from, you can use them as landmine instead. It is that simple.

Landmines have thus been used in many conflicts especially as a means of terror against non-combatants. Some major landmine countries have not entered the relevant international treaties in existence and major producers have escaped the rules and regulations by hiding out under the protective wings of governments, in one way or another heavily involved in the military industry, or its side benefits. The reality is, that landmines will continue to be used as a weapon of choice in many future wars to come, including other 'victim activated weapons systems' including the unexploded bits of cluster bombs.

After conflicts, such munitions sit in – or even on – the ground and wait. They wait until someone ploughs a field or builds a house. Very rarely are they mapped and they make the task of reconstructing already poor and devastated countries almost impossible. As well as all the other obstacles already in its way, landmines also put a brake on development, slowing the task as well as killing and maiming those who would be a part of that process. Horrific pictures of the impact of landmines on individuals are thus only a part of the story as the whole of society suffers.

The aim of the International Demining Group (IDG) is – with local partners – to employ, train and deploy members of affected communities to help rid themselves of landmines and so aid the development process. Creating close ties with affected communities enables IDG and its partners (both National and International) to more effectively place development funding into areas of greatest need and greater sustainability. The organisation has a wide vision which encompasses demining action and development issues.

The last word before getting back to the football shall be with a survivor, Fikret Zahirovic a father of three from central Bosnia (who did almost qualify for Euro 2004), who lost a leg to a landmine whilst out gathering strawberries. "When I think about the man who put the mine in the ground I imagine a man without a family, without anybody. I would say a man without a soul." If you would like more information on landmines, or would like to help, please contact: info@demininggroup.org

Prediction 4

That if England win people will get far too drunk. I know

this is a no-brainer but I mention it with still-painful memories of the day after England's rugby World Cup win. And in case I miraculously didn't manage to mention it anywhere else in this book, I should also note that England won against Australia, even though the latter played their very best and England didn't and even though the referee gave every 50/50 decision – and most of the 40/60 and 30/70 ones too – to the Aussies. And what a marvelous drop goal it was by Jonny 'Is that all that you've got' Wilkinson...

Prediction

That Barry Davies will resort to all manner of crass national-stereotyping (of course I haven't resorted to anything like that in this book) as well as insisting on pronouncing players names differently from all other commentators so that we'll think he's very clever and actually did some research into the language. Alan Parry will describe almost anything as a dangerous cross providing that it meets one exacting criterion, namely that the ball must be lobbing gently into the arms of an unchallenged goalkeeper at the time. Alan Green and Jonathan Pearce will continue to irritate but somehow be regarded as the sort of people the public wants to hear by the people who employ commentators.

Prediction

The Americans still won't get it. In fact there is much they don't get. Actually, if 'Dubya' gets his way, the USA will probably soon reserve the right to intervene in regional 'soccer' tournaments in the interests of 'peace and security', but for the time being they don't get to play in these championships and will be oblivious to their happening save for a few immigrant populations (the Greeks getting over-excited and enthusiastic again, only to be cruelly disappointed!) and possibly a highlights package on ESPN 2. The whole 'soccer' thing just sums it up for me; they play marginal sports like 'gridiron', baseball and basketball and call them the world championships. They are also responsible directly and indirectly for the deaths of countless times more people than all the terrorists in the world put together. Their aid, weapons and political pressure/'sponsorship' result in death, torture, poverty and injustice on a huge scale on a daily basis. Their own society is riddled with greed, guns and great inequality. Their use of resources threatens environmental collapse, but they always just want more. They are responsible for so much wrong in the world and yet dress themselves up in a thin cloak of respectability and piety. Let's hope they never get their paws on the laws of football or we'll have eight seven-and-a-half-minute periods, counting backwards, points for corners, rolling substitutions, goals 10 metres wide, mechanical robot goalkeepers...*[Editor's note: He thought he'd get away with sneaking this in the conclusion, but I'm gonna have to stop him there!]*

Prediction 7

OK, some football predictions at last in which, after my limited 'success' in terms of the play-offs I challenge you to see if you can do better. The scoring works like this:

three points for the correct score, one point for the correct result. Double points if you predict the team not in capital letters to win and they do (i.e. the underdogs). For example, let's take France v England as an example. France are the favourites (disagree all you want: it's *my* scoring system!), so the match appears thus:

FRANCE v England

- If you predict FRANCE to win 1-0 and they do, you get 3 points.
- If you predict FRANCE to win 1-0 and they win 2-1 or by any other score that is not 1-0 you get 1 point.
- If you predict a 1-1 draw and it is, you get 3 points.
- If you predict a 1-1 draw and it's 2-2, 3-3, 0-0 etc you get 1 point.

BUT

- If you predict England to win 1-0 and they do, because you have predicted the underdogs to win you get double points. For the exact score that would be six points. If England won by a different score you would get two points. Does that make sense? There's bound to be some shocks and this system helps reward you for spotting them. OK, so here we go. The matches, my prediction and a space for you to enter my points and your points. (Sometimes the favourites will only be marginal – or you may disagree – but we're all playing to the same rules. You also have the advantage of not making your predictions on a cold December day...unless it's December 2004, in which case you're cheating).

Group A

Match	My Prediction	My Points	Your Prediction	Your Points
PORTUGAL v Greece	1-0			
SPAIN v Russia	1-0			
Greece v SPAIN	0-2			
Russia v PORTUGAL	1-1			
SPAIN v Portugal	0-1			
RUSSIA v Greece	2-0			
Total Points				

Group B

Match	My Prediction	My Points	Your Prediction	Your Points
Switzerland v CROATIA	2-1			
FRANCE v England	2-1			
ENGLAND v Switzerland	3-0			
Croatia v FRANCE	1-1			
Croatia v ENGLAND	1-1			
Switzerland v FRANCE	0-1			
Total Points				

Group C

Match	My Prediction	My Points	Your Prediction	Your Points
Denmark v ITALY	1-1			
SWEDEN v Bulgaria	0-1			
Bulgaria v DENMARK	1-2			
ITALY v Sweden	1-1			
ITALY v Bulgaria	1-0			
Denmark v SWEDEN	2-0			
Total Points				

Group D

Match	My Prediction	My Points	Your Prediction	Your Points
CZECH REPUBLIC v Latvia	1-0			
GERMANY v Holland	0-2			
Latvia v GERMANY	1-0			
Holland v CZECH REPUBLIC	2-1			
HOLLAND v Latvia	1-1			
GERMANY v Czech Republic	2-2			
Total Points				

Disclaimer: I don't really think Latvia will beat Germany, but it would be nice so I thought I'd predict it anyway!

And the Winner is...

Well almost certainly me, but let's just check shall we?

Group	My Points	Your Points
A	☐	☐
B	☐	☐
C	☐	☐
D	☐	☐
Grand Totals	☐	☐

Prediction 8

Predicting beyond the group stage is tricky, but we'll have a go. Success here will obviously be related to your success above, but this might give you a chance for revenge. All predicting to be done before the start of the tournament. The scoring here is quite simple. Award yourself one point for each quarter-finalist you predict, two points for semi-finalists, three points for finalists, four points if you correctly predict favourites France to win, five points if you correctly predict any other team to win, except England for whom you will get six points if they win, for no other reason than this is a whim which just came to me! So, from your predictions above – and using the tournament chart below to help – work out your eight quarter-finalists and how they will match up in the draw. Then decide who will win, what the semis will look like and so on. I have worked through my predictions as an example below.

My quarter finalists: Portugal, Spain, France, England, Denmark, Italy, Holland, Czech Republic. Yeah, I know this probably goes against my earlier predictions in the team sections but football is no topic on which to get consistency of opinion now, is it?

Winner A v Runner Up B: **Portugal v England 1-2**
(one point each if these teams are in the quarter-final anyway)

Winner B v Runner Up A: **France v Spain 3-0**
(one point each if these teams are in the quarter-final anyway)

Winner C v Runner Up D: **Denmark v Czech Republic 0-1**
(one point each if these teams are in the quarter- final anyway)

Winner D v Runner Up C: **Holland v Italy 1-1**
(one point each if these teams are in the quarter-final anyway)
Holland to win on penalties.

So, my semi-finalists:
France, England, Czech Republic, Holland

England v Czech Republic 1-0
(two points each if these teams are in the semi-final anyway)

France v Holland 3-2
(two points each if these teams are in the semi-final anyway)

So, my FINAL!
England v France
(three points for a start for each of these teams which actually
makes the final)

My Final: **My Prediction**

England's run to the final is not wholly impressive.
Much of the burden, especially in terms of goal-scoring,
falls to David Beckham in the form of penalties and free-
kicks in and around the box. In Australia the whinging
Matilda newspapers bemoan the dominance of English
sport in the world. In France *L'Equipe* runs a feature on
England's opening game defeat to France. England barely
get out of their own half, pegged back by free-flowing
French football, and only kept in the game by Beckham's
tireless running, accurate passing to the front men out-

lets and tenacious tackling. England's goal in that game is scored in injury time from a long-distance free-kick from Beckham. So *L'Equipe* have a picture of Beckham under the heading 'Est que c'est tout que vous avez?' (Is that all that you've got?)

Further French taunting accompanies England's route to the final. The 3-0 against the Swiss included two penalties and a free-kick, and the fortunate draw against Croatia which put England through to the quarter-finals was due to an own goal. Whilst the semi-final win against Portugal was always likely to be a case of hitting a passionately backed opponent on the break (Rooney and Owen chipping in) the semi-final was once again settled by a Beckham free-kick and the French mocked and boasted of how they would turn us over in the final.

Indeed, in the early stages it looked like they would do that, scoring after just five minutes through Henry. But back came England through a penalty and then a move of exquisite pace and passing, finished off by a thunderous Lampard volley. In the second half, France seemed to get all the dodgy refereeing decisions and gradually took control. Just when it seemed England would escape and hold on, Terry (in for the disgraced Rio Ferdinand) mis-controlled on the edge of his own box and gave away a free-kick in trying to recover. Henry blasted home with just seconds to go. And so to extra time, where the match went to and fro, but with just 19 seconds left Beckham's half-volley from distance after the ball was laid back by Gerrard flew into the corner of the net. 'Est que c'est tout que vous avez?' indeed!

England win 3-2. (My wife calls this 'footbal w***ing'! And of course it doesn't sound anything like the rugby

World Cup final adapted to football!)

If England do win, I earn six more points. If you predict France and they win, you get just four. If you successfully predict another team to win you get five. If all of my predictions were correct I would have 8x1 point for the quarter-finalists, 4x2 points for the semi-finalists, 2x3 points for the two finalists and 6 points for England winning, making a possible total of 28. Let's see, shall we...

Prediction 9

That even if my startling predictions don't come true, indeed if it is an unmitigated disaster for England, or we lose in the finals due to an outrageous Pires dive (which are only OK against Pompey) then you can guarantee that in 10 years it'll mean very little to you. So just enjoy. As well as England v France, the draw has also brought together the great historical rivalries and animosities of Denmark v Sweden, Portugal v Spain and Germany v Holland. No doubt the Czechs and Latvians would take some pleasure in beating the Germans too! So sit back, relax and enjoy.

Prediction 10

That if we do win we can finally forget about this lot: the 1966 World Cup winning team.[38]

Wouldn't it be nice to forget about 1966 and all that? Not completely, obviously, but if Eng-er-land could only repeat the feat it would be much more exciting than

---

38 This section – with minor modifications – first appeared in Arcturus' 2002 World Cup book and for the very same reason it appears here. We all just need to move on from 1966 and all that, and a 2003 rugby tournament doesn't quite do it!

always harking back to past glories. But until then we must reflect upon the glorious year of 1966 – and not only because the author was born then. No, 1966 was also the year that England managed to do what Spain, Portugal, Scotland and a re-united Germany have never managed to do, and 32 years before the French at that. England won the World Cup! And although the European Championships don't carry quite the same kudos as the World Cup, it would be nice to win them at least once! But until that happens, here's a look at those heroes of 1966!

In Goal
Gordon Banks (Leicester City)
Pub conversations seeking to identify the greatest England XI of all-time will invariably begin with

> *'It's gotta be Banksie in goal.'*

And although some buffoon is likely to add 'but what about Shilton?' they will always and quickly be shouted down in the general consensus that Gordon was great and Banks was brill. When his career was ended by the loss of an eye in a car crash in 1972, the strength of feeling for him was demonstrated as more children sent cards via the TV programme *Blue Peter* to wish him a speedy recovery than ever contributed to the Cambodia 'bring'n' buy' sale appeal or made a pencil holder for dad out of used loo rolls and sticky-backed plastic.

Gordon had modelled himself on Bert Trautmann, the German prisoner of war who had stayed behind after the war and, like it or not, become an ambassador for Germany in the sense that people wondered if the 'Hun' could be all that bad if such a bally hero as Bert was one of them. Banks did a pretty good impression of Bert, although he missed out Trautmann's lunacy of playing with a broken neck. Banks conceded just 0.8 goals a game in his international career. Better still, in World Cup matches Banks let in, on average, less than half a goal a game and even admits to giving himself a really hard time about not saving a penalty from Eusebio in 1966. OK, so his role model Bert saved 60% of the penalty kicks he ever faced but Gordon ought to go easy on himself: Eusebio really was rather good!

In 1972, a little before the car crash, Banks became the Football Writers Association 'Footballer of the Year'. The only previous goalkeeper to win the award was Trautmann in 1956. It was a fitting end to his career, although even without one eye he was still good enough for a couple more seasons in US 'soccer'. But remember, in England's greatest team there's no doubt what so ever, it's gotta be Banksie in goal.

Full Back
George Cohen (Fulham)

George's proudest moment in life came in 2002 when he got through to the last six of Britain's Brainiest Footballer hosted by Carol Vorderman. Although the competition was shrouded in controversy – *Guardian*-reading assassin Graham Le Saux refused an invite – George looked to be heading for a final round confrontation with two Third Division footballers no one has ever heard of until his chances were scuppered by a particularly tricky set of questions on 'The Arts'. Prior to this TV quiz, of course,

George's proudest moment came when he was a part of England's winning team in 1966.

As a player George literally had a life-long affair with Fulham FC. Well no, actually, not literally because that would be as silly as David Pleat (or was it Graham Taylor?) opining that an Italian player in Euro 2000 'literally had no left foot'. For George to have literally had a life-long affair with FFC, he'd have probably had to work his way through Elsie in the tea bar, the girls in the ticket office and today he'd be snuggling up with Al Fayed on a Friday night. So no, not literally an affair with FFC, but he was a one-club man.

Yes that rarest of creatures, a one-club man, the likes of which you don't really find in the modern game, apart from that bloke from Guernsey who played at Southampton. Nowadays Fulham has a range of current internationals including Dutch and Portuguese, but George was still the most recent Cottager to play for England while with the club. Having won his battle with stomach cancer, George now has to live with the shame of being more stupid (though slightly slimmer) than Alan Brazil, who won 'bronze' in Britain's Brainiest Footballer. Also the only Jewish member of the team and uncle of Ben Cohen, winner of the rugby World Cup in 2003 with England.

Other Full Back
Ray Wilson (Everton)

It may well be that poor old Ray, and not John Connelly, is the least remembered of the 1966 winning team, but he was a fine player. Like Francis Benali, (former goalscorer for England Schoolboys) Wilson was once a forward who tried his luck at full-backing. Fortunately he took to the position like a duck to water, unlike Franny who took to it like a cat to water...but bless him, he does try.

Ray kicked off his England career after completing military service in Egypt, making his full debut in 1960 away to Scotland. Without national service he might well have earned more than his 63 caps. Mind you, he might also have turned into the kind of ill-mannered guttersnipe who doesn't know the meaning of respect and could really do with a bit of discipline.

Almost missing out on the 1966 finals with a back injury, Ray went on to play a vital part in quarter and semi-final goals. Whilst not being as famous as Moore and Charlton, both Cohen and Wilson were stalwarts of the defence, who played 28 times together.

1966 was a great year for Wilson, the World Cup being the second time he'd climbed the Wembley steps, having won the FA Cup 3-2 with Everton against Sheffield Wednesday. He experienced a less happy ascent in 1968 as Everton lost to a Jeff Astle strike and his career went downhill thereafter. After captaining Oldham he joined the family firm of funeral directors. Denis Law described him as the most difficult player he ever had to pass.

Vicious Defensive Stopper Type
(Rarely Appreciated – like John McGovern – But Nonetheless Vital)
Nobby Stiles (Manchester United)

Nobby Stiles was born James Alfred Stiles but decided that Jimmy was neither frightening nor silly enough to worry other players. At around 4 ft 7in it is unsurprising that he wanted to be a bit more frightening so he changed his name by deed poll to 'Nutter' B****** Stiles.

Alf Ramsey later insisted he change this to 'Nobby'.[39]

In the 1966 group game versus France, Nobby committed the most horrendous of tackles and was booked. Nowadays of course, refereeing inconsistency means a player can be sent off because the ref senses garlic on their breath and yet another time not even be booked for serious offences like attempted murder. However, in those days, Nobby's booking for a scything challenge was thoroughly merited and FA officials put pressure on Ramsey to drop him.

Fortunately, Alf was stubborn and pompous in equal measure and in a Wenger-like show of loyalty insisted that Stiles (vicious animal or not) played in the quarter-final v Argentina. Stiles proved a hero as England beat those animals from the Argentine (Ramsey, 1966). In the semi-final Stiles was then charged with kicking lumps out of Eusebio (er, sorry 'marking' him) as England won 2-1.

In the final, Stiles' faith never dimmed as he was convinced England could win. By the end he was so tired that he could hardly move, although somewhat unluckily his last ounces of energy were expended in a silly jig caught for posterity by a camera. To quote a phrase, Stiles was a 'son of a bitch but he was our SOB'!

Lanky Centre Half
Jack Charlton (Leeds United)

Although Stiles never became known as 'Small Nob Stiles' for some reason, 6ft 2in Jack did become 'Big Jack Charlton'. In fact he almost became 'Pig Jack Charlton' but the offer of a job with the police arrived just a day

---

39 None of this opening paragraph is true, of course, and Nobby was a magnificent 5ft 5in when fully erect.

after he had already committed himself to Leeds, for whom he made his debut aged 17.

Oddly he was almost 30 before he won his first England cap and that just a year before the World Cup final. A great sense of timing indeed. Jack went on to prove his shrewdness when he became the first man to spot that almost everyone in the UK was Irish (the author is 1/32nd Irish for instance) but that only some of them were good enough to play for England. But that was later.

Prior to his alchemy in Eire, Big – almost pig – Jack played in all six of England's World Cup games with brother Bobby and afterwards travelled to the council offices in their home town of Ashington to receive a gold watch and engraved tankard. Thus the brothers completed a unique double by both monopolising the north-east memento scene and the Footballer of the Year award (Bobby in 1965/66 and Jack in 1966/67).

Jack also did impressions. His favourite was a giraffe (so called by his team mates because of his telescopic neck) but he also did a 'mini Bert Trautmann' by playing (and scoring) on one occasion against Scotland with a broken toe. According to subtle Alf Ramsey, Jack was only picked because he fitted in with a game plan. Harsh though this seemed at the time, the idea that any old donkey could win with a game plan stuck with Jack when he came to manage the Republic of Ireland. Presumably taking the job because of excellent Irish fishing, Jack's tactics of hoofing the ball into corners and then pressing the throw-in succeeded in producing a desperately dull team of Anglo-Irish who did much better than Eire had ever done before.

The Rather More Elegant-Looking Centre-Half
Bobby Moore (West Ham United)

Robert Frederick Chelsea Moore (that is his real name, this isn't a rehash of the Stiles gag) played 108 times for England, 100 of those under Alf Ramsey. His first game as skipper came when he was just 22 as England thumped the Czechs 4-2 in Bratislava. Although playing in the 1962, 1966 and 1970 finals, Moore didn't play a qualifying round for any of these competitions.

Possibly the most famous of the 1966 team (although Geoff and the Russian linesman come close), Moore also enjoyed club success, helping West Ham to FA Cup glory in 1964 and European Cup Winners Cup success in 1965. However, a faultless career on the pitch is often remembered also for false accusations of theft whilst on a pre-World Cup (1970) shopping stopover in Bogota, Colombia. The trumped-up charge saw him delayed for four days before joining the rest of the team in Mexico. Latin American prisons are not the best World Cup preparation, but although England were eliminated Moore looked his usual assured self.

Moore returned to Wembley as a Fulham player in 1975, though by then no longer an England player. Unfortunately in the decade of plucky minnows gloriously winning the FA Cup in red and white stripes, Fulham were unable to join in, losing, perhaps inevitably, to West Ham. After a spell in the US and another season with Fulham, Bobby Moore retired after exactly 1000 senior games. He died of cancer on 24 February 1993, aged 51.

Tireless Runner in the Middle of the Park
Alan Ball (Blackpool)

Radio 1 DJs Mark and Lard often pondered and questioned the managerial genius of Ball, none more so than when he took off a lanky centre forward replacing him with a winger, and when he encouraged his team to time waste even though they needed a goal to avoid relegation. 'Squeaky voiced little t*****' I think was how they put it. However, Ball the manager is underestimated; let's face it, not many men have kept Southampton in the Premiership for consecutive seasons, even if the second was while he was managing Manchester City, who edged the Saints on goal difference for the privilege of being relegated.

But let us instead reflect upon Alan Ball the footballer. Son of a professional footballer, Alan never had any doubt that he wanted to follow in the family business. He was able to fulfill his ambition of playing for England before his 20th birthday by just three days. At age 20 years and 5 days he already had three caps which included a 2-1 win against Sweden.

Alan's triumph is all the more remarkable for the obstacles he has had to overcome. Not just the short, squeaky, ginger ones but also spectacular O level failure. Perhaps this 'lack' in the brain department can explain taking off tall strikers so that the winger you bring on no longer has a target man? But we did say we were going to focus on the player. Coming into the World Cup squad late, Ball played in four of the six games, including the final, where his tireless running made all the difference.

Alan played for Bolton as an amateur, Blackpool when winning the World Cup, Everton, Arsenal and

Southampton. Whilst with the Gunners he is reputed to have stood on the ball in one game, then jumping off as the defender raced towards him, before knocking it round him. As a manager he retained that level of confidence – and always sent out entertaining teams – but alas his skills were more limited. Ah but who cares, he helped England win the World Cup.

Hat-trick Hero
Geoff Hurst (West Ham)

Geoff Hurst was the adopted son of Davinder and Jetinda Jagpal who found him abandoned in an orphanage in Bombay. He came to England with them in 1946 travelling third class on a big boat. Once in England, a playground accident led to him having to have his left arm replaced by one carved from solid teak.

No, of course that's not true but then you're really searching for something original to say about the man. His hat-trick in the 1966 final is the only one to have been scored in the final and is included in a total of 24 goals in 49 international caps. Not surprising that this total is lower than that managed by Charlton, Lineker, Greaves, Finney and Lofthouse, but it is also fewer than Robson (the old war horse) and Platt (the balding horse).

A good player and crucial to the successful West Ham team of the mid 1960s, the ball really ran for Hurst in 1966. Despite the heroics of a goal in the 4-3 win over Scotland at Hampden in only his second international, by the time the World Cup rolled around, Jimmy Greaves had thumped four past Norway and played the first three of England's World Cup matches. However injury to Greaves saw Hurst score the winner against

Argentina in the quarter-final and even when Greaves was fit, Hurst kept his place for the final.

Eight months after the final, Hurst scored another hat-trick in a 5-0 drubbing of France. Wow! When will we ever again see our strikers knocking in hat-tricks as we put five past top European opposition? As seemed fashionable, after spells with Stoke and West Brom, Hurst tried his hand at soccer in the US. He thought it was all over...and of course it was.

He of the Famous Shot
Bobby Charlton (Manchester United)
The incredible esteem with which Bobby Charlton is held is indicated by Gary Lineker's spot-kick against Brazil which would have equalled Bobby's record of 49 goals for England. Instead of blasting home as he had done so many times before, Gary decided to tap the ball to the keeper in deference to Charlton. How I bet Gary wishes that were true, rather than him having stubbed his infamous toe trying one of those 'great when they go in' chips.

Anyway, Bobby played for Manchester United for 20 years and won the European Cup, League and FA Cup with them, averaging almost one goal in three games. With England he won the World Cup and averaged almost one goal in two games. Sir Matt Busby said of him 'he was as near perfection as man and player as it is possible to be.' He received an OBE and, in 1994, a knighthood. Not a bad career really.

Bobby, as is well known, grew up in the north-east where he lived 'in't shoe-box in middle't road'. Whenever he got the chance he played football, usually with a pig's bladder. Of course much of the time he was being pushed up chimneys, with a chimney fire unfortunately burning all his hair off aged 13. His success, in spite of it all, is surely proof that today's footballers are far too pampered.

Bobby's first England goal came against the might of Scotland, only 10 weeks after he had survived the Munich air disaster in 1958, but he did not get picked for any of England's World Cup games in Sweden, 1958. Going on to play, as he did, in 1962, 1966 and 1970 he can consider himself unlucky not to have played in four consecutive finals, but then again it was quite a reasonable career anyway.

Nobby Stiles said of Bobby 'He is the greatest player in the world. A wonderful all-round player with the grace of a gazelle – unlike that clumsy giraffe of a brother of his'. Bobby said of Nobby 'Oh my, oh my, he's the greatest dancer, that I've ever see-een'. Jack said of Nobby 'Wait till I get my hands on you, you short a**** little b*****'. Jimmy Greaves said of Bobby that he 'was the perfect foil, with the strength and tenacity of two men. I fed off him for years.' Presumably he then felt thirsty.

Unsung Hero
Roger Hunt (Liverpool)

Of course Graham Taylor's reign as England manager proved that almost anyone could play for England (and Sven has chipped in with a cap for Francis Jeffers), but before such ideas were fashionable, Roger Hunt was perhaps as unlikely a World Cup hero as England had. Don't get us wrong, Roger was a great player, but being turned down by Bury is a less than auspicious start for any career.

In 1959, whilst in the army near Swindon and playing

for a local team, both Liverpool and Swindon offered Hunt terms. Amazingly, money-bags Swindon offered better terms, but home-sick Hunt chose tiny Liverpool. When Liverpool won promotion to the top division three years later, Hunt scored 41 times. 1962 was also the year of his England debut, as he scored in a 3-1 victory against Germany's second team, Austria. He was then omitted for 14 games before returning and scoring again in a 2-1 away success against Germany's real second team, the DDR (East Germany). In 1964 he scored four in a demolition of the USA in New York, when unlike 1950, England really did score 10.

In 1966 he scored three goals in six World Cup games and his quick thinking in claiming Hurst's 'goal' rather than trying to put the rebound in to make sure was pure inspiration. His intelligent and unselfish football might find modern day comparison with Teddy Sheringham (though not from me) but Hunt's 245 goals in 401 games for Liverpool is almost beyond comparison in the contemporary game. Despite stepping down from international football in the face of press pressure to recall Jimmy Greaves, Hunt also managed more than one goal in every two internationals (18 in 34). 'Sir Roger' as he was to Liverpool fans, was a very, very nice man.

The Other Forward
Martin Peters (West Ham United)
Martin Peters was a Cockney. To Geordies this means anyone from anywhere south of Yorkshire but Martin was a real genuine Cockney, being born within the sound of Bow Bells, having a Thames lighter-man as a father and having rather a thing about jellied eels.

At the 1966 World Cup he played five of the six games, replacing John Connelly after the first match against Uruguay. John Connelly eh? Just goes to show not everyone in the squad was famous!

Martin scored 20 goals in 67 games for England and captained England four times, including the home match v Poland that saw England eliminated from the 1974 World Cup qualifying. Martin's nickname was the ghost, because of his ability to appear unseen at the far post to head goals. But given Nobby Stiles' opinion that he was impossible to pin down, perhaps 'the eel' would have been more apt?

Not Forgotten
Jimmy Greaves (Tottenham Hotspur)
Martin Peters was reputedly traumatised by the fact that his boyhood hero Greaves was omitted from the final. Would England have won the World Cup if Greaves had played in the final? The fact that we don't know means we probably ought just to be grateful for victory. And of course, along with the 11 who played, Greavsie is, at least, remembered... which is more than can be said for...

Forgotten
John Connelly (No Idea)
John Who? Exactly. John Connelly was in the successful 1965 England team which avenged the 6-3 defeat by Hungary. Connelly was picked for the first match v Uruguay but missed out thereafter. He is included here as a representative of all those nearly men. But then again, he actually played in a World Cup finals and he played for England! Until Graham Taylor's reign devalued that

idea, that is something that all those in the crowd would dearly have loved to do...

The Manager
Alf Ramsey

What a pompous big-head! A man of few words, big success and enormous faith in the fact that it had to be 'my way or the high way'. Amongst his most famous few words was his entreaty to his tired players before extra time of the final against West Germany, 'You've won it once, now go out and do it again' he said. And they did.

After a promising start as a player with Southampton, he swapped the path of the good and the righteous for the dark side, represented then, as now, by Spurs. A year later he was a member of the team which beat Scotland to qualify for the 1950 World Cup finals, and at those finals he was a member of the team which lost 1-0 to the United States. Unsurprisingly a man of few words on that particular subject, he was once asked if he had played in the match against the US. He replied that he was the only one who had. There is no independent evidence that he was any better than the rest.

Ramsey was also there, and scored, against Hungary in the famous 6-3 defeat. It was his last international. After thus being involved in the two matches which did most to shatter English football's unreasonable sense of superiority, it was surely only right that Alf ought to rebuild the superiority complex and salvage his own pride by winning the World Cup as manager. Indeed, that England would do so was something Alf confidently predicted when taking the job in 1963.

In May 1965 when England, including John Connelly,

beat Hungary 1-0, the team had a familiar look from numbers 1 to 6. Banks, Cohen, Wilson, Stiles, Charlton and Moore. But the 7-11 selected by Ramsey that day – Paine, Greaves (who scored), Bridges, Eastham and Connelly – all failed to survive through to the final.

As the finals approached, Ramsey settled upon a 4-3-3 formation which saw the team become known as the Wingless Wonders, the phrase capturing the popular imagination in a way that calling them the 'Fluid system with a defensive bias in the context of the era, in which any one of several players can fill the "hole" and support the attack' probably couldn't have.

Alf was one of those people of whom it is said he demanded complete loyalty and respect but offered the same in return. Actually, people were probably just rather scared of him. But arrogant Alf or not, you can't argue with the record books.

Trainer
Harold Shepherdson

England's trainer since 1957 under Walter Winterbottom and one of those people with whom Alf established his famous rapport of loyalty and respect. Harold described the 1966 World Cup as his greatest memory; in fact he was so excited that when England won he jumped from his seat and raised his arms in triumph. Understandable, wouldn't you say? Alf told him to 'sit down'.

Harold Shepherson was awarded the MBE in 1969.

The Star Linesman
Vladimir

They won't admit it, but it still annoys the Germans...

Prediction 11

Whether or not England win, allowing us to let the class of '66 be gracefully forgotten, in answer to the question earlier in the book about when will Northern Ireland ever score again, the answer will surely be in the 2006 World Cup qualifiers, against England!

Final Prediction

If England win then maybe the publishers will ask me to write another book about it? In any case, I hope you enjoyed this one. Thanks for reading.

⚽ **Euro 2004** Schedule

Game	Group	Match
1	A	Portugal v Greece
2	A	Spain v Russia
3	B	Switzerland v Croatia
4	B	France v England
5	C	Denmark v Italy
6	C	Sweden v Bulgaria
7	D	Czech Republic v Latvia
8	D	Germany v Holland
9	A	Greece v Spain
10	A	Russia v Portugal
11	B	England v Switzerland
12	B	Croatia v France
13	C	Bulgaria v Denmark
14	C	Italy v Sweden
15	D	Latvia v Germany
16	D	Holland v Czech Republic
17	A	Spain v Portugal
18	A	Russia v Greece
19	B	Croatia v England
20	B	Switzerland v France
21	C	Italy v Bulgaria
22	C	Denmark v Sweden
23	D	Holland v Latvia
24	D	Germany v Czech Republic
25	-	Winner Group A v Runner Up Group B
26	-	Winner Group B v Runner Up Group A
27	-	Winner Group C v Runner Up Group D
28	-	Winner Group D v Runner Up Group C
29	-	Winner Match 25 v Winner Match 27
30	-	Winner Match 26 v Winner Match 28
FINAL		**Winner Match 29 v Winner Match 30**

Tournament Matches ✪

Date	Time	Venue
Saturday, 12 June	5:00pm	Oporto
Saturday, 12 June	7:45pm	Faro-Loulé
Sunday, 13 June	5:00pm	Leiria
Sunday, 13 June	7:45pm	Lisbon
Monday, 14 June	5:00pm	Guimarães
Monday, 14 June	7:45pm	Lisbon
Tuesday, 15 June	5:00pm	Aveiro
Tuesday, 15 June	7:45pm	Porto
Wednesday, 16 June	5:00pm	Porto
Wednesday, 16 June	7:45pm	Lisbon
Thursday, 17 June	5:00pm	Coimbra
Thursday, 17 June	7:45pm	Leiria
Friday, 18 June	5:00pm	Braga
Friday, 18 June	7:45pm	Porto
Saturday, 19 June	5:00pm	Porto
Saturday, 19 June	7:45pm	Aveiro
Sunday, 20 June	7:45pm	Lisbon
Sunday, 20 June	7:45pm	Faro-Loulé
Monday, 21 June	7:45pm	Lisbon
Monday, 21 June	7:45pm	Coimbra
Tuesday, 22 June	7:45pm	Guimarães
Tuesday, 22 June	7:45pm	Porto
Wednesday, 23 June	7:45pm	Braga
Wednesday, 23 June	7:45pm	Lisbon
Thursday, 24 June	7:45pm	Lisbon
Friday, 25 June	7:45pm	Lisbon
Saturday, 26 June	7:45pm	Faro-Loulé
Sunday, 27 June	7:45pm	Porto
Wednesday, 30 June	7:45pm	Lisbon
Thursday, 1 July	7:45pm	Porto
Sunday, 4 July	**7:45pm**	**Lisbon**

GROUP A

Portugal ☐ ☐ Greece
Porto, Sat 12 June, 5.00pm

Spain ☐ ☐ Russia
Faro-Loulé, Sat 12 June, 7.45pm

Greece ☐ ☐ Spain
Porto, Wed 16 June, 5.00pm

Russia ☐ ☐ Portugal
Lisbon, Wed 16 June, 7.45pm

Spain ☐ ☐ Portugal
Lisbon, Sun 20 June, 7.45pm

Russia ☐ ☐ Greece
Faro-Loulé, Sun 20 June, 7.45pm

GROUP B

Switzerland ☐ ☐ Croatia
Leiria, Sun 13 June, 5.00pm

France ☐ ☐ England
Lisbon, Sun 13 June, 7.45pm

England ☐ ☐ Switzerland
Coimbra, Thu 17 June, 5.00pm

Croatia ☐ ☐ France
Leiria, Thu 17 June, 7.45pm

Croatia ☐ ☐ England
Lisbon, Mon 21 June, 7.45pm

Switzerland ☐ ☐ France
Coimbra, Mon 21 June, 7.45pm

GROUP C

Denmark ☐ ☐ Italy
Guimarães, Mon 14 June, 5.00pm

Sweden ☐ ☐ Bulgaria
Lisbon, Mon 14 June, 7.45pm

Bulgaria ☐ ☐ Denmark
Braga, Fri 18 June, 5.00pm

Italy ☐ ☐ Sweden
Porto, Fri 18 June, 7.45pm

Italy ☐ ☐ Bulgaria
Guimarães, Tue 22 June, 7.45pm

Denmark ☐ ☐ Sweden
Porto, Tue 22 June, 7.45pm

GROUP D

Czech Republic ☐ ☐ Latvia
Aveiro, Tue 15 June, 5.00pm

Germany ☐ ☐ Holland
Porto, Tue 15 June, 7.45pm

Latvia ☐ ☐ Germany
Porto, Sat 19 June, 5.00pm

Holland ☐ ☐ Czech Republic
Aveiro, Sat 19 June, 7.45pm

Holland ☐ ☐ Latvia
Braga, Wed 23 June, 7.45pm

Germany ☐ ☐ Czech Republic
Lisbon, Wed 23 June, 7.45pm

GROUP **A**

	P	W	D	L	F	A	Pts

GROUP **B**

	P	W	D	L	F	A	Pts

GROUP **C**

	P	W	D	L	F	A	Pts

GROUP **D**

	P	W	D	L	F	A	Pts

Quarter-Finals

Quarter-Final 1

| | □ □ | |

Winner Group A   Runner-up Group B
Lisbon, Thursday 24 June, 7.45pm

Quarter-Final 2

| | □ □ | |

Winner Group B   Runner-up Group A
Lisbon, Friday 25 June, 7.45pm

Quarter-Final 3

| | □ □ | |

Winner Group C   Runner-up Group D
Faro-Loulé, Saturday 26 June, 7.45pm

Quarter-Final 4

| | □ □ | |

Winner Group D   Runner-up Group C
Porto, Sunday 27 June, 7.45pm

Semi-Finals

Semi-Final 1

| | □ □ | |

Winner QF1   Winner QF3
Lisbon, Wednesday 30 June, 7.45pm

Semi-Final 2

| | □ □ | |

Winner QF2   Winner QF4
Porto, Thursday 1 July, 7.45pm

Final

Winner SF1

Winner SF2

☐ ☐

Subs

Subs

Goalscorers

Goalscorers

Euro 2004 Winners